CAELESTIA JUDICIUM

Heavenly Judgment

A Vagabond's Journey

S.C. deSTEIGUER

Available as an ebook

ISBN 978-1-968640-10-1 (Paperback)

ISBN 978-1-968640-11-8 (Hardcover)

Publify Publishing

Lampasas, TX 76550

contact@publifypublishing.com

The Spiritual Truth

We are not mortal humans seeking to have a spiritual soul experience while on this journey.

We are spiritual souls seeking to have a mortal human experience as we've been manifested in this journey.

That! ... is the challenging element in this life.

Dedication

"Humanity's mortal journey walks through the eras of time with no bonded guilt of judgments or shackles upon each step. Life's manifest is God's doctrine, granting all free spiritual credence. Weep, not for me, for I am free with my spiritual conviction."

The Universal Spirit does not judge us:
Judgments are human inventions,
A means to compare, contrast, and control.
As we judge ourselves against
Artificial and often idealistic standards
Of perfection, morality, or truth.
As youth fades and time brings changes,
We may change many of our present opinions.
So, let us refrain from setting ourselves up.
As judge of the highest matters.

Plato

Disclaimer

"The pursuit of imaginary or indoctrinated faithful hypothetical esoteric philosophies, or comparative correspondence with the realization in societal theistic mystic ideological theories, and or that of the sciences remains an interdisciplinary conviction for oneself to contemplate without judgment or self-guilt."

Contents

Preface

Spiritual Heart of an Author

*A*n ideological concept of life is a variable. It exists in a form that evolves from an inaugural source. A created variable of matter is an event of universal aggregation of molecules, creating atoms and ions, and evolving into functional entities through anatomical physics. Created matter, a functional entity, can evolve for betterment purposes based on the mutation adapting to its energized environment and potentially infused influences with other variables. Evolution cannot exist or evolve without first having been a created entity. Therefore, arguments of sciences and theistic ideologies that creationism must come first before evolution can proceed, whether creation is from a cause of superior effort or an energy event causing an agglomeration, herein known as an originating instant by its Creator. How perfect or imperfect such a creation is to be determined, for perfection can be infinite yet undiscovered. Regardless of beliefs in faith and or scientific consequence, the consideration is an interdisciplinary fiction or non-fictional theory that best satisfies an intellectual soul as opted without indoctrinating convictions for the reason of domination.

As significant functional living matter is created—birthing, indifferent to any others, having similarities in molecular chasm structure—it will evolve into its identifiable mass, here forward known to become a specific species of its own. One natural, primal species evolved into a more archaic hominid as a living being. It was anatomically functional in all aspects of senses, with limited abilities other than to exist most simply. A remarkable transformation occurred as evolved hominins, the greater species, achieved functional senses that became cognitive in thought, influenced by actions and reactions to natural or imposed emotional events.

The ability to use the senses, more so the sense of peripheral nerves sending impulses of an event inflicted on the simplest of brains, gave an understanding of either discomfort or pleasure. This in itself was a basic foundation of senses and cognitive sensibility of simple thought mannerisms of emotion using feeling and or imagination in early humanity, creating forward thought to become curiosity that collectively became knowledge of life's means to develop.

It was the early hours of the morning, the first day of Autumn, to be exact, in a dimly lit birth room in a hospital, now long demolished with time. Entering and observing life for the first time, what is now known to be a new spiritual mortal journey. Raised by a family that would open the doors to the world of adventure and knowledge of life's cultures. Later adolescent years, sitting in the kitchen chatting with my mother my experience at birth and explained as remembered.

Completely astonished by the disbelief expressed, I described the room perfectly at that moment of entering life. It was not for many years before I was introduced to and even knew of life as a journey given to you by God to conduct tasks during this mortal life, not knowing of possible past life(s). To a young person, such matters were absurd and completely hierarchical to the instilled dominance of a religious environment in the teachings we were raised to believe. In this, religious domination lays the disguised considerations to an inner spiritual belief. Not to ever know of these subjective matters in life, rather only that of the strict indoctrination of religious teachings. Raised in a part-time participating Episcopal High Church of England, we were indoctrinated to believe whatever the King James Bible version demanded, and the Pope of the Catholic church was to be the absolute word of God.

So many earlier scripted philosophies of God's will have been reputed and ignored, and not acceptable; why? I ask. What was truly scripted, we were not to know? I was never truly exposed to the heart of down-home Hell Fire and Brimstone orating, as many were in their lives, no matter what religion was being followed. We were told one must fear the wrath of God, but praise him if one expects to go to heaven when one dies. The question is...Why would I have to fear someone when I am expected to praise for my life's journey and fear him? I never determined within my spiritual beliefs such an issue. Further, to give earnings to a religious sanctum in belief, to able the entry to an eternal life, is so untrue to God's intents. Or even support the unjust (Bellum Sacrum), religious wars of indifferent belief in God, when all humankind is children of God, and each holds in their spiritual souls a deep love for their creator. I believe soul and heart in God and give praise to him with thanks and questions each day again for the wonderful life he has sent me to live. Of course, as we all know, life and our tasks are not easy, but then again, it's as difficult as one chooses to make it at times, including the outward boundaries of influences we allow to interfere.

Having traveled the world with my family at an early age and been exposed to many cultures' theistic behavior and astonishing ideologies, some more dissatisfied than others, which always seemed to be praising a higher spirit of some kind. In my younger working years, I again traveled extensively throughout the world to many countries and listened to such diverse cultures speak of God, a creator, and, again, a higher spirit to be praised. Of course, in most theistic ideologies, each has its rituals of prayers and praises for assumed dominance over all others.

I found most interesting in these times listening to elders of different cultures and theistic philosophies, such as the native chief in the Amazon jungle, speak of the praises of a creating higher spirit to guide him through life and again, the elder desert Bedouin in the Sahara Desert and a true desert camel herder in the Rubal Khali, an empty quarter of the Arabian desert, all ever so wise in their spiritual world of peace. All spoke of God or their spiritual creator in many languages with different names, but always as a higher spirit.

These conversations continued throughout other parts of the world while traveling and gaining conceptual knowledge of the Creator and the conceived purpose for us as mortals in this life. At this time in life, I discovered that, yes, life is a journey to learn that a Creator has given a manifested journey for a purpose, and all humans are to endure a journey of their own for many reasons of certain indifference left to each individual to understand and pursue.

Granted, as children of our Creator and as brothers to all humanity, we strive as hidden angels to support our brethren through many hardened journeys with a hand or two. Those who arrive in disbelief of our creator shall only endure a difficult journey, only to have learned what disbelief is and what the absolute truth is upon their return to God's eternal home, the afterlife. That purpose was to live the exact life you are in while learning the knowledge of the given wisdom to all things created and the beauty of nature's mandates, while all the time accepting our Creator to be referred to as God's will of essence and existence to embrace your inner soul for which life carries.

For more than 70 years, this mortal life, which I must say has certainly been an adventure far beyond another's imagination could ever conceive, was lived as others have their own story to tell of their journey. This has given me a guiltless, peaceful world, realizing I am here living a mortal life as I had most likely several times before in other times, possibly for other cultural humanistic reasons. Certainly not a theologian nor a theistic scriptures scholar or biblical orator by any means, although enjoying reading translated ancient Apocrypha scriptures of times and, for sure, the indoctrinating pseudepigraphal writings to gain insight into world ideological theistic cultures.

I had gathered consciousness to realize not to desire organized theology or allow it to dominate or its alluded guilt, but rather to believe in God for myself as his child to enjoy our uninfluenced relationship. I learned this exceedingly early and have lived well without the rhetorical rituals of complete indoctrination for domination. Nor that one religion any better or ever be dominant over the other, nor ever shall be, no matter the ignorance of theological wars that proved nothing except the obliviousness to God's will for humankind. Theistic philosophies can offer the peacefulness and gracious manners of life's guidance when left to one's free will to believe as God intended. God is always within you through this life's journey to guide you with spiritual strength, bear the hardness of times, and peace within your soul with forgiveness and love to all. As spiritual souls born into a surrogate mortal human life, we were sent here to live and learn from the character that we shall live to be in this journey, following four very simple edicts God has provided us to live by as best we can. Years ago, knowing it was inevitable to draft this story, I seemed to instantly mind titling the book Caelestia Judicium, a continued vagabond's journey.

It was not until recently that, while writing the text, I realized the spiritual soul's life was not about judgment but learning about humanity's excelling evolution of civilization. All the answers came from studying and researching various subject matters of the historical philosophers of all centuries past and self-witnessing many cultures throughout the world. Leaving a simple explanation written in the introduction for all to read, learn, and guide their way through life.

What you are living is life itself for the reason it is. Understanding the true journey requires you to consume the exquisite nature of the four veils and edicts through prayer, asking God to guide you.

"May God bless and guide each of us as we journey through this mortal life as the spiritual souls we are."

For the Love of Humanity

The historical injustice and unkindest act of humanity is the infliction of periconceptional ideologies and social prejudice upon its brethren. The horrors and unrest which in itself has befallen man and other creations of God, the near devastation to nature, the reluctance to encourage knowledge and wisdom, and most of all, the absence and false testaments of spiritual belief in God himself. This has belittled humanity to the simplest of creatures, trying to dominate the other. Overcoming such perils and adhering to the true word and guidance of God, which he intended you to journey through in this mortal life, will require you to step out of the realms of this life's domination of indoctrination, where you shall become estranged from society but gain the wisdom and enlightenment to the truths of humanity and the real natural world of true spiritual belief in God and yourself.

CAELESTIA JUDICIUM

An Inauguration of Life

A s the universe comes into being, from an orb of the first day to the present, a nebula and cosmic events and evolutionary intervals evolve into their origins, creating the centuries of a living planet. The sheer magnitude and beauty of this process, with no perceived evidence of a physical Creator, as perceived in portrayed more than a mythical scripted ideological judgment throughout humanistic civilizations. What is true of imperative logic, or an elected testimony, is the interdependent evidence of "the created, by a creator's, desired more so as 'God,' cause." Reach out into the emptiness of the cosmos, touch the textured asteroid and comic elements to be of this earth, view all living fascinations created, and sense the spirited soul within quenching the breath of life, for each is an ecological ingredient of the creator, ex nihilo, the "ALL." We, the spiritual souls on this mortal journey, knowing a higher spirit, our Creator, accept more graciously a natural, unembodied, celestial, immutable spirit who exists in a gnostic, unmeasurable dimensional universe. A perceived signified spirituality to become commonly known as God to "All," who created the universe as an openness with no inauguration or threshold to measure its nucleosynthesis infinities. The universe gives reflected lighted darkness a beauty to its fullness, with the spheres and luminaries echoing the center of the cosmos.

The universe is not without symmetry of organizational hierarchy of asteroids with atoms, causing circumstantial discharges expressing collisions of infusion and immersion from its physical centrifugal cosmic force, creating planets with opposing gravitas poles. How the universe began and why it's here is an intrinsic, timeless, universal principle of cosmic phenomena valued and viewed once as a Ptolemaic system, seemingly unknowable yet evolutionarily becoming scientifically definable.

Perfection is not infinite, and yet many universal principles remain a mystery. The universe's evolution, with its myriad of existing planets, stars, and wonders, is not fully comprehended in the simple universal mentalism of energy, power, and matter or the superstitious theistic verses. In a sequence of analogous positive and negative frequencies of inner planet volcanic turmoil, gravitational forces infused colonizing outward planetoidal geometric stratigraphical growth, occurring as they did by theorized nebula causes of celestial element events from the universe. Possible accretion events as cosmos spheres gave credence to the universal velocities as the gravitas alien their orbital Heliocentric placement from one place to another around the Sun, center, as others are in an obliquity rotation about each other. Through the universal evolution of cosmic debris, an embodied planet, and ancient lava hardened into Obsius, became known as Pangaea (everything, Mother Earth). Created over billions of years, with an atmosphere nearing suitable oxygen-isotope conditions accommodating living organisms from different elements, a gradual cosmic nucleosynthesis evolution from cosmic debris infusions.

This gradual evolution, guided by the principles and eternal laws of life's evolving causes and reactions, is a testament to patience and appreciation for the process of life's existence. Therefore, in the relation between ancient steadfast theistic mythical ideology, seven days, and evolving scientific theories, it took billions of years to create a cosmic ontology entity developed as the motion of the evolutionary process. For the advancement of our scientific understanding, it is crucial to separate ancient myths from the realm of knowledge. With an unbiased approach, delving into the truths of the universe's rhythms and polarity provides greater clarity. This is not to dismiss the possibility that certain events in theistic apologetic scriptures might have occurred. Modern science has, in some cases, transformed these mythical events into tangible realities, as evidenced by descriptive writings and pictorial wall and pillar markings. Our intellectual curiosity and pursuit of knowledge are crucial in this endeavor, as they lead us to a deeper understanding of the universe and our place within it.

Science evolutional interventions and evolutionary interventions shall never defeat each other; rather, they exist in mutual understanding as science seeks the realization of universal origins and interprets theological edicts as pearls of scripted, limited mystic concepts with precise evidence, as faith praises the natural evolution of all created. Our creator, whom we commonly refer to as God, offers two focal reasonings in the Four Veils: Creations are for science to discover its wonders, not to compete with, as spiritual faith is humanity's eternal celestial understanding of the creator's creations to sustain civilization, not that of imaginary mythical theistic ideologies. As reflected in the scrolls of scripture, the presumption that God's perfection may be absolute is compared to humanity's phenomena in the evolution of humanity's actual belonging and differences.

Throughout the millennia, civilizations have asked the question with such a misunderstanding because theistic theories cannot explain the universe, the "ALL." God created man first in the simplest form, only after the prehuman Cambrian evolutional period, later in the Cretaceous period with earthen metabolic biochemist elements existing with self-replicating RNA and DNA elements evolving into a great-minded species as each hominid form brought forward new experiences of knowledge, rendering a stigmergy of future knowing and wisdom as the earliest Earth's monitor and concierges. As the significant functional living matter is created but indifferent to every animalistic creature, many similar molecular genetic chasm structures will evolve into an identifiable mass, known as an algorithm of biochemical-genetic mutation of a new species of its "own" nature.

Over millennia of evolutionary adaptation, a primal mutated species evolved into the form of archaic humankind as a living being. Is it possible that the creator created man as he did, extremely different from other living animalistic creatures? Yes, only to be a primal genius profoundly different from the earthen, elementally, molecularly, to live in unison upon the earth. Why did God create more than one archaic hominid human-like erectus bipedal homo, only for one to develop into modern humans, the homo sapiens species?

All different from the Hominin, possibly two to three million years in time, an earthen epoch, Pleistocene known to date, perceived first as the Alkebulan (ancient Afrika) and considered, this far as the first human species group in the evolutionary cycle. Each human-like form, a species of the identifiable preciseness of its somatic change, was biologically molecular and physically unique to its habitat in the evolutionary geo-stratigraphic earthen interval period for a reason.

The Earth itself continued to evolve with changes in its moment ever-accruing resemblance and has yet to end. In modern studies, many species created did not survive in a misanthrope environment. Each of the earlier species' senses and emotions contributed to a cognitive and phylogeny adaptation in an inductive idiosyncratic behavior by "natural cause/event," consciously expressing its simplest daily experiences to the continuance of humanity's greater survival, sometimes in barbaric violence in its evolutionary period. Somatic flexibility was an absolute in an environmental evolutionary period. An unnatural event in this period was not nonexistent; why? Because a natural event is based on earthly causes of its elements, not by unnatural invented circumstances. The unnatural events were and are developed by modern humanity, not nature. All of nature's events are natural causes for evolutionary purposes. Each species of its period may have struggled to survive in the other's earlier environment. The differences in the species' environmental periods led to the continuation of discovery.

Science has evidence of the ending periods of one species and the beginning of another, which led to genetic lineage alterations and a shift in the evolution process. Some interrelations led to the extinction of one species, leaving traces of DNA in future generations of species. As hominids' physical and mental development evolved, so did their ability to comprehend thought to use rocks and tree sticks as tool for survival. They were very protective pro-social to the inner tribe, which established a culturally specific hierarchy, and anti-social to the outsiders' hunters and gatherers. This in itself creates a lineage of branching social and biodiversity hominid evolution.

Cognitive simplicity-minded inductive and deductive reasoning, curiosities, sensibilities, and a natural biochemical algorithm function evolved forward shall be an epicenter to human actions and reactions to a "cause of an event," as learned. All other senses influence psychosomatic thought patterns in unison with the anatomic organs. As continuously being entirely convincingly self-sufficient by nature becomes inquisitive, a heuristic human evolves into knowledge-gaining wisdom, and everything becomes ecologically minded as interdependent, the "All."

The human attitudes and developed influences familiar to one evolving human group were unfamiliar to the later evolved generations. However, the perceived uncovering of history gave insight into such influences in earlier behaviors, as proven by the remaining tools and weapons used for survival, for each may have contributed to different objects.

Through the millennia of evolution with intellectual and cognitive development, egotistical syncretism, human pro-social algorithmic interaction, understandings of thoughts, and then beliefs became dominant over individual life. This became a serious stigma of hegemony to the point of a custom of a Hobbesian-like nature, demanding followers to adhere to the felt vibration of an "event by cause." To this epoch point, man had not yet discovered the inner spiritual soul of his own as himself.

The earliest means of imposing simple-minded, invented superstitious concepts from these events and causes facing social consequences, a form of early group/tribal morality, may have been the beginning of a possible primal polytheism, the Gods of different events, with implied quilts deriving as a traditional theistic orality mindset. Therefore, an "event" had its own conceived God(s) to adhere to, if necessary, to live through an occurrence. Unaware of psychological instincts, simple-minded occurrences perpetuated pre-religious events, mindfully accepting that all occurring events had Gods when unknowingly none existed. The historical phenomenon remains: if God purposefully deferred the knowledge of his universal existence with the first archaic human, only to allow its conscience to evolve from an "event by cause" inspired polytheism into acceptable predominantly monotheism in a Godly universal presence and creator of the "ALL"? "Let the ancient thunders of storms begin, for the God of lightning created it." Praised with rituals of archaic inflectional sounds and signals, possibly the beginnings of an oracle language.

Only one species survived the millenniums of human evolution timeline, as perfectly as modern man would like to think of themselves; modern humankind, homo sapiens, has a more extraordinary continuous evolutionary process and intellectual, rational ethical consciousness. So proven, the modern species shall carry a minute DNA percentage lineage of one or two ancient species. Even in modern cultural times, many simple self-minds, still an "event by cause," are necessitated by a society's orality-diverse translations of God(s).

God gave the created earthen element, now a living human species, an evolved mortal, and his celestial, spiritual soul in his conceived likeness. All to live independently of the physically embodied creature, never to die as that of its host physical human body, performing in the earthly biological mortal essence, acting as a surrogate conduit for the spiritual soul on a manifested journey. The spiritual soul, with its human living duration as its evolutional anthropomorphic physical character only to leave it to earthen nurturing decaying matters while itself returns to the eternal dimension in a manifested end of its time.

As mortal humanity further evolves, the curiosity of tomorrow's humans rises. For, without creation, the evolution of the universe could not organize the phenomena of numerous chemical and biological environmental mitigation factors of occurrences creating differences in various living species. Shall there be a more intellectual mindset, a superior human, or the evolving artificial post-human comprised of earthen elements with conceived human intelligence, one without spiritual credence? All mortal humans remain humble in a means of faith in a divine God within the unembodied, immutable spirit, a creator of the cause of the first universal event.

Earthen elements have created all as the Creator intended his creations, with pervaded infused spiritual souls governing manifested journeys as planned from the earliest of species. Anatomically functional in all aspects of organs with interrelated psycho-physical senses, first with limited mental abilities, other than to exist most simply developing consciousness within its environment to survive.

As humankind evolved, humanity achieved a more practical conscientious sense, currently discovered and identifiable as the five senses, evolving into the simplest of cognitive inductive thought through the effects of actions and reactions to occurring natural or imposed inner emotional "events." The purpose of the abilities is to consume the senses for inner peace and or primal survival instincts within their environments.

For somewhere in the time of humanity, an acceptance of spirited beings and mythical gods is predictable by the occurrence of natural events as perceived. A time of evolutional periods with limited conscious knowledge shall coincide in an acceptable harmony of wisdom, creating a mindset of philosophies and theories. Possibly a ritual of theism in a tribal environment, establishing a possible spiritual behavior. Inner spirituality, different from collective theistic minds, became self-liberating from indoctrination and dominance, believing in their creator with all their soul and body with the spiritual gift to life. As in all ages of humanity, the barbaric political theistic scriptures are never-ending in continued brutal civilizations.

Regrettably, when faith is derived from theoretical philosophies, it can be misinterpreted as a belief that one must only have faith if one is obedient to an ideological environment. However, faith is a deeply personal covenant, a belief in God, the ultimate creator, who provides solace to my human soul, free from the influence of external judgmental pressures or guilt. This freedom from external judgmental pressures in faith liberates us, and we strive to empower ourselves to form our divinity within God's universal veils.

Intellectually, in various respects, post-structuralism toward theological ideologies for those who no longer adhere to the dogmatic, rigorous, or resonant religion's rituals of the altars, the pulpits, monasteries, or prayer towers, instead live an emancipated covenant journey with our creator of true mortal life. Their spirited souls wept from the pain of the imposed evolution of humanity's civilizations. The functional human body in the mortal form uses its evolutionary created character only to exist as an utterly applicable entity with the spiritual soul given by God to develop as a continuity of "ALL" human beings, known as "self."

Life is a continuous journey, with its various phenomena and values influenced by the past, present, and future. This journey begins before our mortal existence, in a future known as the vibrations of life, in God's likeness as an unembodied, celestial, immutable spiritual soul within the eternal dimension commonly referred to as heaven.

Our mortal life, a creation of God but not in his likeness, but only as he imagined each of our species to be for a reason, is the present evolutionary life as we know it, in a manifested journey as the species character we are. The afterlife, or history, is the return of the immutable spiritual soul to the divine eternal spiritual life, healing from the perceived brutality of a mortal human journey, and possibly being assigned to a new journey in another life. This emphasis on the continuity of life's journey serves to reassure us and instill hope in the future.

Over the millennia of history, humanity's solid and diverse cultures exploited their differences in theistic ideologies, faith, and spirituality. Therefore, the determination of an accepted narrative is left to one's own heuristic devices of a theistic or methodical mindset. As all have learned through mortal lives, religion is a basis of theistic ideological philosophies and canons of historical scriptures, following particular sects and relinquishing guarding the only creation codes needed for humanity, the four veils.

In this, the religions and their beliefs are said by the indoctrinated populous to be absolute as the only one demanding the governing statute over all others, and they shall not hesitate to massacre others who do not acknowledge their likeness. This is how polytheistic means and misunderstood monotheistic beliefs lead to uncivil cohesion, causing xenophobia and radicalism, and possibly the annihilation of cultural humanity.

The ideologies of theistic idiom doctrines and rituals ministered customarily to indoctrinate cultural obedience for the passive calmness, peacefulness, and inseparability amongst the weakest. In real life of the time, spirituality is considered the inner soul that dwells within you, the enlightenment of the natural earthly element body, and the spiritual soul manifested by a higher spirit, our creator. Many great children of our creator, his sons, have journeyed as spiritual souls into the mortal human life to orate with inflections' tongues in diverse cultures of spiritual similarities of God's peaceful veils, only to have many misscribed for purposes of dominance in future generations. Still hidden in verses are words in a theistic faith so that God's codes can be known, giving the true knowledge and wisdom to evolve through this mortal human journey.

As we evolve into individual humans on this mortal journey, guided by our holy-spirited Creator, our spiritual soul acquires and comprehends the environments and their habitats for human civilizations. This understanding is not just for the resolution of life itself but also for contributing to the evolving existence. For millennia, ancient man lacked the scientific knowledge to comprehend the actuality of earthly evolution and human origins, instead adhering to a theistic, obedient, mythical conception. For in this mortal human life, as we are journeying, we look not for spiritual experience except in meditating and praying for guidance in our creator's interdependent natural truths.

We, as spiritual souls, seek the journey of reasoning in our various mortal human lives, living within the constraints of a timed evolutionary civilization. This is our challenge. In truth, as spiritual mortal humans, we are not bound by the obedient guilt of mystic theist ideologies or the mindless denials of anti-theists. We reject the contradictory and unclear conceptual definitions of God presented by these groups.

God shall always remain to each of us as our creator and a spirit of natural, unembodied, celestial, immutable spiritual phenomenon. But one we all, in our hearts, bodies, and the souls of our minds, refer to in meditative thoughts and prayers for strength, guidance, and reverence during our journey. For only as our spiritual souls return home to our eternal life shall we truly be acknowledged.

"I am one with my creator, God."

There is Life before Life, the future.

*T*his raises the question of having a life before mortal life; there must be the existence of Life before mortal Life, a spiritual soul's life is eternal, and a mortal human life itself exists in an interval period of a journey. This concept of life as a journey is not just a philosophical idea but a profound truth that demands our contemplation and introspection. For all unembodied spiritual souls, lives are celestial and dimensionally simultaneously lived. Therefore, there is a spiritual life and mortal physical life, a sequence before mortal life and after death, where the unembodied spiritual soul returns to the eternal dimensional spiritual, celestial world as manifested. To ensure an appropriate understanding, humankind must be of the spiritual mind, body, and soul and know there is a much greater spirit in the universe, a oneness with our creator, that gathered the universe's heterogeneous masses of particles and created all to give life to all things. Therefore, those of humanity who accept a higher immutable celestial spirit as the creator and understand and appreciate the historical evolution of systematic developments through the millennia to better understand creation with an open, conscious mind, with faith and evolution appreciated jointly. For each, make both true and not without the other. Scriptures of all theistic philosophies and envisions, as told, of our creator, the great powerful one, created the heavens, earth, and eternal spiritual soul, a being alike in the theistically known Creator, unembodied celestial immutable likeness.

With no eugenic considerations, that all humankind and living matter is created of bio-chem earthen elements, for mortal life is given to each living hominin being the surrogate conduit for the spiritual soul, part of our creator, which is within us to strengthen and experience this journey. A spiritual soul is seeking a mortal human life journey. This remained a phenomenon when the first spiritual soul became consciously evident, contributing to consciousness in their thinking in this earliest period of prehistoric hominin; Australopithecus, a man-like creature closely related to us, the only true homo sapiens.

Life is a manifested journey for a reason, a reason to experience mortal life. This journey is guided by the extraordinary spirit of God, transitioning the spiritual soul into the mortal life dimension, creating eternal spiritual life upon the earthly human journey. The selected nurturers for this particular spiritual soul's mortal life journey play a significant role. They guide and shape the journey, living and humanly guiding the spiritual soul. The lifestyle and environment in which the nurturers (parents) live are also known for a reason, as the environmental lifestyle corresponds to the determined manifested human life for a given cause for the spiritual soul. The evolution of the holy spiritual soul, an immutable naturalistic spirit, shall become God's manifested human, a being that embodies the divine qualities and characteristics of God, using the espousal of biological DNA and chromosomes, creating the human parental characteristics, and receiver for birthing.

The other sometimes may proceed as mentally dominant, creating an imbalance in existence only as it is manifested. In many mortal lives of the past and continuous shall be abnormalities to human life.

Look not upon such brothers, children of our Creator just as you, in an ill will in societal environments, but rather, this is their journey as manifested, as yours shall be yours, as any journey will unite many spiritual souls regardless of their environmental beliefs as one expressing their mutual love of life and emotional love to each other.

As mortals, nurturers conceive you as their own through the divine intervention of God. The inception, whether desired or not, is a force that falls against the natural laws of a spiritually given life, for only God can decide its course. The progression, known systematically to human knowledge, is a result of the wisdom of those who seek knowledge and wisdom of conceptual means and birthing. Human intimate conception between God's humankind's genders, male and female, is a natural spiritual enactment of integrating the developing process of biomolecules into a cellular architecture of organs. The male delivers the sperm, and the female offers the egg. The egg meets in the female fallopian tube for fertilization, where the sperm enters the egg. Sometimes, eggs can bifurcate into two, creating two children. The mortal body is just that, a human body with functional organs that mechanically perform the total body operation and physical anatomical architectural character of a mortal body for this life. The fertilization process causes a blastocyst and implants itself into the walls of the uterus, becoming a living embryo.

The infusion of the divine spiritual soul is a transformative event, turning a developing organism into a complete living being. True life begins when the spiritual soul enacts the heart and mind in the mortal body, akin to the moment when God breathed life into humanity. The mother, as the first to feel the life of the spiritual soul, welcomes a new child of God. The spiritual soul brings an energy and power that allows the body to function as a complete living being.

With spiritual characteristics filled with emotion, sensitivity, thoughts of knowledge, and the nutritious system grows the mortal body whole in God's eye as a human, originally from earthly elements. During the journey of the spiritual soul in the mortal human, the earthen elements influence can be attacked by either parenting mortal humans, causing imperfection in the organic mass of the body. In turn, when the development of a new mortal human is enacted before birthing, these outer earth elements may cause difficulties and an unlikely body development and a discard of continuance in birth. Therefore, a new mortal life has begun, a heartbeat has instituted its function, and its development in time is birth as a mortal living humankind being. A birthed human life is a specific life's journey to begin as manifested.

The established environment, responses, and reactions shape most emotional development. Our environment can significantly influence the dynamics and outcome of our lives, for better or for worse. This realization invites us to reflect on our environments and their impact on our lives.

A Spiritual mortal life, the Life of a living being.

Mortal life is born into a world so different from any previous journeys once lived, for each life's journey shall be manifested for diverse lessons in different nurturers' environments, spiritual soul seeking mortal human life experiences. At an infant's age, learning of life's existence through absorbing, formatting, and environments shall be taught and guided by the nurturers, known as parenting, with the influencing unit as a family with love. A child's reasoning for this life's purpose is consciously unknown, not yet exposed, as boundaries and limitations are set within the living environment in which they may live. As the mortal human evolves in age and then adolescence with emotional and civilizations influences, experiences come into the chartered path. The overt and covert curiosity mindset absorbs its meaning of growth into a purpose of life's journey that will begin to prevail, for all lives are lived for the betterment of humanity, whether known through this life or not. This is not to say some journeys of spiritual souls as mortal humans may be prodigies in their human character and understand a perceived journey very early into the human experience.

Mortal humankind will come upon others and walk through their lives with biological brothers and sisters, and in-kind reach out their heart with a life's blessings, as they too shall smile in their soul of love and in-kind give theirs, no matter their environmental theistic indoctrination. Life shall be endured by learning to accept and understand that there is a manifested purpose for this journey and seeking its meaning through mortal life's path, no matter its life's labor. The journeys are the duration of living as they shall be experiencing the purposes of human life, with the lessons as manifested.

This life is planned to seek, find, and understand, gaining knowledge of the lessons and tasks once never experienced through pasted travels. In all the while of endurance, each shall summon our creator in prayer with praise for the guidance of his spiritual knowledge and following the teachings with truth, no matter the differences in tongues of God's words without dominance as that of the Four Veils and Seven Sands.

Daily life experiences rhythmic conscience vibrations that shall reveal new lessons about humanity and civilization's behavior and emotional spirituality. Realizing the divine essence and purpose of the journey with an understandable peace, bringing a balance of confidence. He who seeks knowledge shall discover the wisdom in building stones with steps to creation and nature for the enlightenment of the spiritual souls of this life and the creator's spiritual soul within you. Life's journey will bring the joined family and friends traveling in their journey seeking different enlightenments. Family is the warmth of strength to endure on all journeys. Hold the firmest loving belief and integrity in all humankind's hearts next to God for this blessing given to humanity. Expect outer influences in mortal life, such as indoctrinating theistic ideologies of philosophy, political encouragement of domination, and awkward character friends contributing to human behavioral actions and reactions. The path you choose in not accepting outward insecurities molds your truth, and such obstacles shall be overcome in this life's journey.

Some will also learn to love and respect their friends and teachers, who have more significant influences to ease and support their journey with wisdom. In an unknown silence, our Creator has given human life with an intellective spiritual guide to convey messages to the mortal's spirit for conscious contemplation of heavenly morals of right and wrong that only the mortal may decide in each step: know thyself. The spiritual principles seek the peace-loving and kind purposes of all for your individual mortal life, with your influencing factors not offsetting the path of the manifested life.

The influx of ideological indoctrination can always dominate the mind of life and cause influences accomplishing distortion of the human conscience's free will and limit boundaries because of social and inappropriate political civilizations and theistic indoctrination. At the same time, intellect, cognitive thinking, and overt curiosity shall always open the door to knowledge, wisdom, and appreciation of nature's mandates for a more accurate, better life during this journey. Having no conscience of life before life, the influences of spirituality, theistic beliefs, and nonbelief will have a significant role in a life's journey as each shall always prevail, dominant over environmental conditions of thought. This has given life's journey reasons to think of life after death from historical stories told through the centuries of humankind. There are three basic categories of human-minded thoughts regarding influences on indoctrination. One may be the absorbed mind completely dominated by indoctrination, which thinks it is the absolute only path, an almost neurotic state.

One may find oneself in the position of the 'inconvenienced mind, 'uncomfortable with the dominant indoctrinated environment. Another may be in the mind of listening with yet unconvincing interest, as the third is an inconvenienced mind without accepting the dominated, indoctrinated environment.

An absorbed, indoctrinated mind will stay entirely within the dominant boundaries, as there is nothing more to guide it. Hence, what is commonly ministered theistically and referred to in the world of hellfire and brimstone as bringing in the sheep, the heathen masses?

Experiencing the outer realms of harsh covert influences, the use of guilt and unwarranted societal judgments is only a creation of the mortal human mind for the dominance of those weak in their spiritual understanding and freedom of belief in God. This is a ubiquitous experience through centuries of misunderstood faiths and the purpose of indoctrination. Our Creator only gives mortal humans the right to believe in him straightforwardly, free-mindedly, not that of imposed, egotistical, hegemonic social dominance.

The greatest philosophical lecturers never rose to prominence with an unconvinced mind that is cognitively related to the influences of life's destination. Still, skepticism may or may not allow the influence to guide them completely. A non-acceptance mind sensation of being unensouled moves unaffected by the influence and continues rationally evaluating and abating cognitive thinking to life's purpose and character. This is also the invisible, silent spiritual guide in action with the mortal human. The unensouled mind, despite its lack of acceptance, remains resilient, inspiring us with its strength in the face of influence.

Each shows the most straightforward vulnerability of influence acceptance and the possible foundations of their reasoning toward life after death and possibly life before life. The truth of life after the "death" evolved from theistic and spiritual foundations on chiseled mud-baked tablets and character itching sketched as scriptures through history, to profoundly continued indoctrination through civilizations' environments for centuries. The simplest form of indoctrination in theistic ideology for life after death is evident in the old and new ideological chants of hymns, prayers, mantras, so scripted, and other theistic documents scribed through the centuries of humankind, promising the return to universal, eternal dominion. Has this happened?

This is possible from eyewitness accounts of out-of-body experiences, also known as near-death voyages. Once spiritually transcended after mortal life, no divine judgment is to come, as theistically indoctrinated into one's mindset. There are only prolonged healing periods for subsequent abuses of many kinds to the spiritual soul incurred during mortal life. Knowing a human's journey shall end one day, and the spiritual soul will return to the heavenly, eternal dimensional environment (Caelus) for eternal vibrational enlightenment. The return is not as the human physical character prevailed in its mortal life of scriptures. Still, rather, it is in a divine, immutable, unembodied spiritual non-density existence, possibly resembling, in a manner, the human character lived. It's crucial to consider the personal narratives of those who have experienced near-death or out-of-body experiences.

These personal narratives, often overlooked in philosophical discourse, can provide invaluable insights into the perceptions and experiences of individuals in this dimension and beyond.

Life after Life, Death of the Mortal Being

*D*eath to all mortal beings is consistent no matter who one is or how long one shall be a mortal living soul within humanity. The planned end of your journey shall come, for not everything living is immortal. No mortal shall know how it comes unless closer to it or an earthly event or civilizational cause will end it, or even fortunate enough of natural causes, to the end, or even in a sudden death concern of just or an unjust cause.

Deaths are seen of others through one's journey, with expressed spiritual sensitivity of emotional bereavement for those known losses. Occasionally, a spiritual soul only, never the full physical character form, by a cause in-kind, may experience an out-of-mortal-physique experience and see the insights of guardian angels in another dimension. Then only to be accepted and transcended to heaven, or not accepted and returned to their mortal life in human form to complete the manifested journey, to continue for other purposes. Humanity has theistically expressed great near-death experiences as a bardo and or period of purgatory through the millennia of civilizations with wonderous, scripturally defined narratives of beliefs only for dominance, not for spiritual reasons of truth.

The physical body structure and organs cease to function when the cause of death ends the journey. They no longer function as the mortal physical body and become inert matter, returning to their origin upon their demise, earth, referred to as dust to dust in theistic terms. Humanity respects the physical death of a body by encasing it in a coffin and laying it into tombs, graves, or repositories, burial in its silence, only in time to re-nurture the earth.

The spiritual soul immediately transcends, leaving the mortal physical body, which refers to the theistic mythical resurrection of the spiritual soul with the physical body in a short period, is untrue. Many theological theories ruminate, as in ancient history, that the actual physical body matter transcends in its entirety, along with worldly possessions, as was once believed in ancient periods. Evolution and archeology have proven this untrue by discovering ancient graves containing remains of the physical body matter and ancient possessions.

The heavens of spiritual guides and angels know the expected times of transition, and pleasing with a joyous spirit accompany the spiritual soul through the Kavod, returning to the Olam dimension for healing from mortal human life. There may be other mortal lives to live in other times, as there will surely be a spiritual life before life to live as well.

Birth of a Spiritual Soul

In the heavenly dimension, the spiritual life we are blessed with is a divine gift from our creator, God. Spiritual souls, as unembodied derivatives of the universal Holy spiritual soul, "the ALL," carry a profound sense of divinity.

The spiritual soul enjoys an endless depth of loving togetherness and indulges in a concept of blessed consummation as immutable spiritual soul images, possibly Aristotelian ontology. For this, the truth of being created in

God's image, an immutable spiritual soul that is like our Creator, is a gift of God.

This is not the case with the myths believed to be in human form, as the chosen human nurturers, father (spiritual male) and mother (spiritual female), are created from the bio-chem elements of the earth for mortal humans as a conduit for the spiritual souls' mortal human life journey to come.

The heavenly, eternal birth of a universal spiritual soul is sacred to heaven and unknown to the human species. It is a segment of the All-soul. Therefore, it is indifferent to evolutionary concerns and developments. It is born to purely spiritual, heavenly mothers and fathers, holy spiritual souls.

The infant spiritual soul is lovingly nurtured by other spiritual souls and angels who are well-versed in life's development. In heaven, these celestial beings, both young and experienced, attend lessons of wisdom for the betterment of our Creator.

They learn from the teachings of the sons of God, the many prophets, and returning spiritual souls who once journeyed through mortal life. Only later did some ministers of God's veils and principles become immortalized by humanistic societal civilizations. Born spiritual souls are given as a heavenly gift by the blessings of our Creator, Father of "All."

Spiritual souls are raised in the genuine belief of God's spiritual laws and veils with life principles only to be made ready at an acceptable impermanence to journey into mortal life, living and applying such edicts, comprehending the experiences of mortal life. Knowing the circumstances of the required disciplines needed from a mortal journey, a spiritual soul can only be birthed through a mortal human Mother and father's biological conception.

The characteristics of the mortal parents, who are also on a journey themselves, must align with the specifications and disciplines needed for the new spiritual soul to manifest on its journey. Some spiritual souls can be born into unpleasant environmental lives as mortals, while others have a much more pleasant experience. Mortal life is born into a specific character in which the journey is portrayed, some with physical or mental impairments, all for a reason, and to understand a certain profile of mortal life.

Within the physical nature, the spiritual soul depends upon the mortal life of parents, mother, and father, with different anatomical and biological genes, half of one as that of the other. This is the basis of the spiritual soul's life in reasoning to journey through mortal life.

As planned, one may journey many times as different characters and learn many other lessons from human life experiences. Such journeys are pleasant at times. Then again, many can be less unpleasant as one chooses to use such edits in decisions about confronted mortal affairs and can change the environment of one's life path. A significant reason for mortal journeys is not limited to the lessons a spiritual soul endures.

But further enable support and constructive contribution of manners in the evolution of humanity upon our creator's earth, its development, and care. With God's immutable spirit approval, the supporting angels and archangels plan the spiritual soul's journey. A society shall not know or understand the complete truth of mystical theories of spiritual soul life and its exact character's purpose until the spiritual soul returns.

There is no judgment of humanity's civilization's wrong occurrences, referred to as theistic sins and laws, and extended goodness to humanity. Eternal Heavenly life's concerns are with the accomplishment of lessons manifested during the mortal journey. All spiritual souls return.

Spiritual Guides and Soulmates of Mortals

Spiritual Guides

God has provided so much for the life of mortal souls while enduring an earthly journey. Yet, many need to be made aware of the spiritual guides. They may be referred to by many as guardian angels, with them unseeing and deaf to their existence as an unembodied celestial, immutable spirit.

A spiritual direction can be one of two entities: yourself from another simultaneous dimension or an angel unknown to you. Spiritual principles send eternal messages to the mortal soul in making decisions for the character it portrays. These signals or messages of acceptable and unacceptable measures in life and conditions to better the mortal life journey. Does mortal life hear these messages? Only those knowledgeable regarding existence and who meditate can listen to the enlightenment of their inner heart and soul.

Not all will or can listen to the inner soul. For one time, if not many, the spiritual inner voice of your guide or maybe a once-known, now-lost acquaintance spirit may speak to you. Nevertheless, those who know the mystical listening methods seem to move forward in their journeys with less vexation than the many who turned to silence their minds.

One hears unexpectedly many times without acknowledging the inner thought or outward vibration. Throughout human history, many have been sent on a journey of ministering, teaching the philosophy of meditation and enlightenment, knowing one's spiritual soul, and learning to listen. Ask, and thou shalt receive from those who know. As written, 'the lips of wisdom are closed, except to the ears of understanding". Blessed be the relationship. Always know that the inner spiritual soul does speak to each of us in a manner of conscience.

Soulmates

What and who are soulmates? There can be several definitions of what a soulmate may be. The first of soulmates most known is the heavenly soulmate, where two spiritual souls in heaven are very close or possibly attached in some divine manner and endure the most loving, inspired relationship, so blessed by God and all in heaven.

If one of the spiritual soulmates has to depart to a mortal journey, it remains possible that the other either stays in the eternal life of heaven or may, if God decides, transcend to mortal life as well. In this case, the two spiritual souls are born into separate environments, or of the same, and possibly be each other's mortal brother and sister, sister and sister, brother and brother, or even meet during their journey in manifested emotional similarities and become mortal partners or remain as friends.

Either way, because of the nature of their journey, the two soulmates shall always be together in understanding and belief in support of the other in a very spiritually-minded manner. It is not uncommon that if one passes and has transcended to the heavenly dimension, the other's bereavement may cause God's allowance to end their mortal journey and return them.

Therefore, soulmates, heaven, and mortal life are essential to any spiritual and human life. Although in many cases, some must journey alone without the heartened accompaniment of a soulmate.

Divine Healing is Non-Judgmental

*I*n spiritual life before human life, a spiritual soul preparing for the transcending and infusion into mortal life, a precise schedule of subjects is encouraged as learning instruments and guides to establish a manifest for the human life's duration. God, our unembodied, celestial, immutable spirit, acknowledges each life, believing in Him with all their heart and acceptance of creation and the edicts of nature for survival and existence as human beings, discovering their inner spiritual souls while on this journey and better understanding the journey's purpose.

Further, God has given the spiritual soul the ability to become aware, a consciousness, and evolve into these human civilizational habits with grace and the edicts of spiritual etiquette behavioral experiences when circumstantial cycles and forces of nature, implying a gain of knowledge to become wisdom during this journey. Evolving as a human being through the journey may occasionally be unpleasant, as again, it shall be most pleasurable in understanding the fundamentals of the experiences.

Not to say all is well, but for courageous journeys, expect the challenges that can be misguided and misled, or solely in righteousness with pride, knowing their accomplishments in the journey. Incorrectness is inevitable where correctness is absent, known as a human nature occurrence for a reason.

Each shall not endure divine judgment as alleged by human civilizations' theistic mythical indoctrination, for it is a human creation establishing a measurement of status and control to seemingly justify a construed ideological ill truth of morality or immorality to assure a hegemonic society. Judgments are man-created; one's experiences during a journey are not of spiritual judgmental concerns, as it remains more decisive whether designed, manifested lessons in spiritual principles and guides may have been cultivated. Returning to the spiritual dimension of eternal life is a healing experience from the harshness of mortal life endured, no matter the simplicity or severity of one's mortal position during the journey.

In all mortal theistic ideologies and philosophies, there is a paradox of ministered controls established to dominate a sect of humanity employing harsh indoctrination, establishing a mindset. For centuries, humans have lived by these rules to control culture and instill false beliefs about eternal life and God by establishing pure guilt as the underlying cause. Fear not, for all is untrue to spiritual life as that in a heavenly, eternal dimension.

Universally, the mortal human being does experience the external forces of the cosmos at times, as millennia of ancient cultural, mystical ideological philosophies have the means to align with time. The external cosmos force influences energy to the mortal human soul in its silence. The purity of divine healing after mortal life with God and the archangels, higher spiritual angels, shall be a spiritual soul's most sacred experience before re-entering the eternal, immutable spiritual soul's dimensional heavenly life.

The Four Veils and Seven Sands of God

T he Four Veils of our creator are very contented for mortal human life to accept, and those who choose to believe in reducing the tendency of entropy measures. First, our creator asks humanity to believe in him as not being of naturalism but rather in actual celestial, immutable, unembodied spiritual existence. He is in an Olam dimensional universe of his own. The archangels in the heavenly dimension are potent protectors and healers who oversee the angels and spiritual souls. Sometimes, perform healing when a spiritual soul is out of alignment with divinity and needs assistance to ascend to higher well-being. Each archangel has a particular area of care and support in assisting in the four veils and seven principles and laws of mortal life while enduring their journey. The seven principles also provide one or more archangels who can guide a mortal's life during the journey. Our creator has only invited humanity to understand the interdependence in the Four veils of truth and the seven sands of principles to better their journeys. The archangels and spiritual guides are unembodied, celestial spirits unknowingly present to the mortal soul spiritually at all times.

Many sons of our creators previously traveled through their respective journeys of time orating our Creators' words and philosophies, leaving scripted lyrics chiseled onto tablets and gematria scrolling papyrus encryptions for humanity in the millennia for beliefs in human harmony, peace, and occasions.

The history of humankind through its centuries of civilizations has shown many differences and unrest in nature to God's guided creations. Leaving humanity with a more significant need for sincere sustenance in this dimensional journey, for the journeys are of limited time to the universal heavens of eternal life. The great temples, cathedrals, spiritual domes of stated life, pillars, and tablets of scriptures with carved commands and the ancient philosophies of peaceful verses were never enough to bring harmony to all humankind. Many who believed so knelt in a meditative prayer of thanksgiving unto God for his greatness and the sons who came as his teachers and philosophers. Many teachers throughout history saw the inconsistent insight of ministries of the hegemonic falsehoods to be aware of god's truths and philosophies. Open thy eyes and listen to the true words of God's creative wisdom expressed by many who saw the truth.

"For he who listens shall become wise to the unreal and falsehoods of darkness, but know the truth."

Proverbs from Humanity

Ephesians 6:12
"For we wrestle not against flesh and blood,
But against principalities, against powers,
Against the rulers of the Darkness of the world,
Against spiritual wickedness in high places."
From the Pavamana Mantra

Brihadaranyaka Upanished
Lead from the unreal to the real.
Lead me from the darkness to the light.
Lead me from death to eternal immortality.
Let there be peace, peace, peace.

"I am my Creator's child, not a slave to the humanitarian hegemonic ministered illusions of mystic falsehoods."

The Four Veils

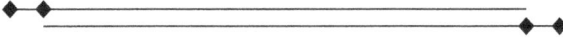

The First Veil.... Believe in Me

Our creator, God, invites humanity to believe in him during their journey, for he is omnipotent in their creation of everything. Therefore, each spiritual soul created shall be in the likeness of their immutable celestial, spiritual existence. For each shall transcend to a spiritual mortal human life with the spiritual laws as a character analogous to their birthing nurturers to journey with them. Therefore, believe in me with all your hearts as your Father, creator, and all things; pray and meditate with me for guidance and well-being, knowing I am there. I shall hear your open worldly praise unto me with grace, and the silence of your smiles with answers to your concerns of many verses in all faiths in meditative prayer await you.

The Second Veil....The Gift of Creation and Nature

Observe all around you and understand Nature so beautifully created and provided to nurture your journey with divine balance and substance for life. Praise each day and respect all that shall offer you to sustain your journey wisely. Share the abundance of wisdom in nature and its nurture with your fellow brethren in expressed grace and praise, thanking God for all. The breaking and sharing of its bread and drink shall bring gifts of the giving and a balance of abundance with integrity.

The Third Veil....Knowledge and Wisdom

The divine kingdom of knowledge and wisdom so freely gifted with conscious curiosity, the principle of creation in earth's dimensional formation with nature and truths of human life, one shall evolve undefinably. To remain creatively open to the world and life shall reward the abundance to oneself and the evolution to tomorrow's world you shall bring forth. Therefore, speak with truth and praise God's gift so given with each step forward in freedom, every moment with confidence through this mortal life in belief with his guidance and assistance of knowledge and wisdom with vision.

The Fourth Veil....Believe in Oneself

With inner knowledge and wisdom of the created and life itself, be at peace with a rested mind and enter the inner world of meditative consciousness enlightenment, knowing your spiritual soul, hearing the silence of thy self-speak the belief in your journey and God's inner gifts to the living. The harmony of self-spiritual enlightenment shall give divine strength of outward peace in life's boundaries of trusted openness through environmental endurance, all without emotional guilt and invariable judgment to society other than thou self. Thyself-acknowledged love is invigorated and translucent to all humanity.

The Seven Sands

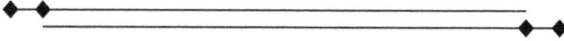

*T*he Seven Sands, referred to as principles and universal spiritual decrees presented by the Creator, are as ancient as humanity's existence, of the mystic philosophical teachings for humanity's respect of guidance for peace and understanding of himself within the created. First, having adhered to and believing in God's Four Veils and the truths of daily existence, one can have a reconcilable understanding of the evolution of human life. The teaching of these veils and principles has been handed forward through the human millennia by the arch angels and many sons of the creator to humanity, not in a celestial mystical manner, but in a guiding purpose of spiritual wisdom with means of curious knowledge for the wisdom it shares as inner gifts. We give praise to the faiths that espoused segments, if not all, such veils and principles of the great prophets known as Abraham, Moses, Jesus, and Mohammed and the great enlightened philosophers of Hinduism and Buddhism, Hermes, Socrates, Plato, and many others for that of the peace serving Yahweh and the council of Elohim, the great ones.

The First Sand of Life....Knowledge and Wisdom

In its simplicity, our creator gave each human an active intellect of proficiency, with cognitive thinking ability utilizing the spiritual soul as its inner self of greatness. As that of the sacred pillar of strength assisted by Uriel, the archangel guides a given cause to the rest of the mortal body and its meaning as created.

A cognitive thinking ability provides the integrity of curiosity, inductive reasoning, a purposeful thought purpose of an unknown event, in or an outside active mortal life, "a cause." An external cause, as any, shall exert the power of wisdom on a matter or sight of the universal existence as seen.

In doing so, the captured event of the human mind brings curiosity to its conscience. The extended thought of events enlightens us to know what is, why, and how. It shall remain a phenomenon until the reasoning, through inductive or deductive reasoning, assesses and determines what is possible. All created is considered a phenomenon to human life until evolutionary conscious thought is applied with a current ability to discover the what, the why, and the how of a caused event and its purpose.

From the mental curiosity assessment, knowledge is gained and, in time, the wisdom of understanding the action of recurrence or close similarities. The wisdom of the evolved knowledge assures humanity of how to accept a cause and accommodate its occurrence and its changing appearance and purpose in an environment. The evolution of curiosity to gain understanding and wisdom shall evolve in the aspect of interdependence, the ALL created.

Humanity's greatest fear and tragedy is the misconstrued use of expertise, whether a matter of fact or philosophical thought. Humanity is responsible for maintaining the integrity of knowledge and wisdom for harmonious balance and life's confidence of freedom to excel in civilization into the future.

The Second Sand of Life....A Togetherness of Opposing Likeness

Existing life as created, curiously seeking its truth, is a universal phenomenon until the perils of conscious awareness awaken the understanding of natural laws of existence and inaccessible pragmatic pieces, if not all of the wonders, evolve its purpose. Each existing and non-existing cause, a phenomenon, is a positive and negative different dimension until the applied universal laws of knowledge are in place and the ability to communicate and understand opposites.

Applied knowledge to ancient discoveries is math, arches of geometry, the distance of objects, and measurements of time, whether existing open time or measured time created by the simplest of civilizations. The universal laws provide the inner secret knowledge of opposing likeness for a disciplined balance and gifted creativity. Gabriel assists in communicating the messages of mental guidance from our creator to unlock a phenomenal discovery to evolve the corresponding teachings of opposing likeness in all encounters.

The Third Sand of Life......An Inner Pulsation

The universe, like everything, including mortal human bodies, is in motion. Nature's growth of all nurtured foliage moves in motion. The motion of all things is the existence of its evolution for continuance with life from its beginning to its last moment of decay. The same applies to all living particles from the cells of all creatures with limbs of large foliage.

The vibration of such movement is the continuous energy sensitivity creation of an inward or outward motion of expressed confidence.

The influence of an outward direction is the energy, from silent to non-silent interference. Such disturbances are universal in the cosmos, everything. Through the evolution of curiosity and gained knowledge, wisdom has provided humanity with the understanding that even as the universe is in constant motion, creating its form of vibration by the most uncomplicated force of rotational centrifugal sensitive force assisting gravity, it can have a universal influence on other created objects within its orbits.

The most straightforward observation known event of an outer vibration force is the effect of the Earth's rotation on the oceans and seas of the Earth's tidal basins. The most effortless known power is the inner body relations of nerve vibrations to impose acknowledging pain or pleasurable sensations to the human body, the truth of expressed sensitivity. The mental pulse of excitement or displeasure by inward or outward events of cause, an experience such as spiritual vibration or emotion in the peacefulness of prayer, so guided by the archangel Selaphiel.

The Fourth Sand of Life....Divergence

Humanity's intellectual mind, created to maneuver with thought and curiosity to gain knowledge for actions of wisdom, can be curtailed in moments of truth and non-truth, or opposing opinions of an event's cause. This is all part of spiritual laws, a cooperative, sensitive balance of proper, acceptable discipline. Hot and cold liquids are equal in a cause but different in their degree of polarity, the same as the truth of an event.

There can be two opposing sides to everything, large and small, darkness and light, noise and quiet, again positive and negative, and right and wrongs of civilizations' indoctrinations of truth and consequences. The archangel Raquel brings the justice of harmony to betterment, as Uriel also assists in the knowledge and wisdom of understanding the environment of truth and non-truth.

The Fifth Sand of Life....Regularity and Succession

The whole physical, mental, and spiritual soul of a human body's conscious function in succession with a movement of regularity. Mutual compliance is its harmonious rhythmic balance to a successful life.

The direction and succession of a functional life move from one place to another, considered a lower and higher plane, changing the polarity of the human function of a physical, positive, mental, or negative state.

Again, there is an inner plane of cause as there is an outer plane of reason, or all can be an inner-related plane of reason. Humans have knowledge and understanding of the environment, which influences their rhythmic self, either inner or outward. This can change the succession and regularity of his physical, mental, or spiritual life by migrating to another environment suitable for peacefulness and growth and reducing gravital influence.

The archangel Selaphiel supports prayers that balance spiritual equilibrium, and the archangel Uriel assists in understanding the wisdom of the stability process of changing environment planes.

The Sixth Sand of Life....Reason and Consequence (Action and Reaction)

In the laws of the universe and manifests, God has decreed that all spiritual souls who shall transcend for a mortal spiritual journey will experience a cause, whether by natural action or phenomena, until defined through knowledge as a cause. The human spiritual soul shall not only share the event but will react sensibly to the event, known as an effect or emotion. As in prayer, the depth of emotion creates the inner reaction of feeling its sensation. Each reason has a manifested purpose, experience in an event, to learn and understand its meaning, and a rationale of stability.

The emotional expression of sensitivity and the mental effect upon the mortal spiritual soul is a lesson learned. No such causes are by chance. All are manifested for a purpose, not by chance but by the cause of natural universal law. An action may present itself as emotional or realistic relative to life's environment and atmospheric conditions.

A phenomenal action is considered until evolving knowledge and wisdom provide evidence of the action's defined purpose. The archangel Barachiel assists in overcoming displeasurable reactions or any obstacles created by an act, bringing life back into its lovely harmony.

The Seventh Sand of Life....Humanity (masculine and feminine)

All of humanity is our Creator's children, the sons and daughters, one of masculinity and the other of feminine nature, known as the only genders.

The purpose of "being" for both can be a multipurpose intention: to be partners as nurturers for future generations, or as soulmates, or in a kind relationship within an environment. God gave his likeness to his children only in an immutable spiritual soul in the eternal heavenly world. He made all of humanity from the mutual earthen elements as he saw best from earth's environment, giving credence to the theistic term from "dust to dust."

As the spiritual soul is to transcend to a mortal soul and journey, the manifested purpose being born into a mortal life through selected nurturers (parents) providing the means with the feminine partner (mother of mitochondrial, mtDNA) collectively in a mutated union of cells and DNA, the Y chromosomes from both contributing parents to create the physical characteristics for a mortal life, as the disciplined freedom at the beginning of all humanity. Through this administration, God decides if the character, now physically resembling both parents, shall be dominant in a masculine or feminine nature, based on the dominance of either parent or the intended journey of the spiritual soul. The chosen mortal gender's physical body shall have both masculine and feminine cells. In contrast, only one shall be the dominant in appearance and energy in character over the other, as that "All" the great spirit who created nature.

The archangel Raphael is always assisting with the preparation of spiritual souls transcending, and when it is infusing during the development of human birthing. Archangel Raphael is very much involved in God's children's healing, physical care, and spiritual growth. The character of mortal life shall experience ease at times in nature, but can also be unpleasant in their environment.

For the Love of Humanity

The historical injustice and unkindest act of humanity is the infliction of periconceptional ideologies and social prejudice upon its brethren. The horrors and unrest which in itself has incurred upon man and other creations of God, the near devastation to nature, the reluctance to encourage knowledge and wisdom, and most, the absence and false testaments of spiritual belief in our Creator himself. This has belittled humanity to the simplest creatures attempting to dominate others. Overcome such perils and adhere to God's accurate word and guidance, which he intended you to journey through in this mortal life. This will require you to step out of the realms of this life's domination of indoctrination, where you shall become estranged from society but gain the wisdom and enlightenment to the truths of humanity and the real natural world of true spiritual belief in God and yourself.

The Vagabond's Celestia Judicium

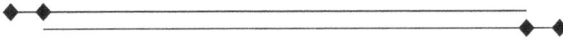

The Return Home

Comprehension of The Last Mortal Journey

I was awaking in a beautiful mid-morning crisp air with an abundance of sunlight. Finally, feeling rested, I knew I was in my eternal home after a long mortal journey, visiting many souls in other centuries. Most pleasing was that I no longer appeared as a journeying vagabond and was myself again. Heaven is the most wonderful, fulfilling dimension god ever created for all of his children. We, the angels, love being here in our home for eternal life. I sat awhile out on the veranda, breathing in the air and reflecting on the warmth of sunlight, relaxing and meditating my mind on the past journeys and gathering my thoughts to relay to the council of archangels my actions of opinion toward the people I had met, even more so from my perspective on earth's condition and the evolution of the human race as a whole in the many generations through the centuries.

What I may think of Earth in the centuries to come is whether humanity will continue to evolve further into a more meaningful intellectual being. This visit was more difficult than visiting earlier human societies in the millions of years and ancient millennia before.

Early man was neither aware nor made aware of a higher spiritual Creator. Yet, in their forward periods of evolution, God wanted man to learn from life's experiences and develop as the human homo species evolved, learning the earlier wisdom of survival in an early brutal world as a being with other created Godly hominid species and earthly creatures and nurturing creations.

With so many obstacles and barriers to overcome with their human socialistic barbarity, genocide, and unjust wars of false holiness, their concerns developed into believing that an actual one God exists, rather than a polytheistic ideology. With so many found beliefs, indifferent philosophies, and indoctrinations of rituals for strengthened domination and rising collective organized groups creatively referred to as religions, each with its distinctive symbol. They worshiped and prayed to a symbol, even to conceal themselves behind its shadows to perform deceit and falsehood of supremacy amongst humanity. As so many others have evolved into excellent, peaceful, caring persons, most profound in divine faith and devotion to God, believing in his principal universal edicts in teachings and lessons for life learned as humans venturing through their mortal journeys. I knew I was in for a long session of questions and expressed opinions that certainly would take great thought and energy from me to be fair but trustworthy, no matter what I said to be heard or not heard, for it all shall be told.

Later in the day, I walked into the great hall of the archangels, all seated in their robes of God's authority around a gothic-like marble table, waiting for my entrance. As I entered the room, all the archangels stood and applauded me with beautiful smiles for carrying out an incredible journey that was needed in their eyes and God's wishes. I felt very humbly honored by their recognition and approval of my success.

We all sat at the far end of the table where each could see me clearly and hear my words for a word they shall undoubtedly hear. Gabriel, the lead archangel, along with Arial, asked me to take this journey and opened with comments to better explain the purpose of the trip over the different centuries and meeting the people I did for a reason. As an angel serving God and the archangels of heaven, I have been unquestionably faithful and served in many journeys through the centuries from the beginning of humankind in mortal life to learn faithful lessons from civilization, working with my brethren as humanity, guiding them as well through their journeys. Even from the birthplace being created with his blood, God, our creator, in an image God willed, has perfectly created the greatest, the homo sapiens, over thousands of earth years, so different and nonlinear to all anatomical physikos forms from other creatures created. To witness the evolution of humankind, gather himself into a curious being of nature, and multiply using the creation edict with a mindset of curiosity about all things to survive. To see his actions of regular earthly events, thought to be of

55

harmful intent, and thought of as spirits or outward gods, which he gave unwarranted sacrifices as an insidious means of relief and peace, only later with consciously come to understand differently.

I even saw the evolution of inner spiritual growth in humanity's quietness, the most straightforward meditation in thought, and discovering the peacefulness of his soul; God had given him to learn and love for himself, and the silent spiritual guide became known to him. The evolution of his mind's curiosity gathered the encouragement to migrate throughout the lands of this created earth to survive and venture into a very wonderous divergent world.

In centuries that came, the evolution of humankind ventured far from its original habitat of birth, the cradle of humanity called Afrikus. They were seeking and experiencing Earth's many differences, arid winds, and ecological structural standings as nature changed with plant and animal domestication providing suitable existence with dwellings and nurturing foods. Only to further develop a mindset in communications, forming the simplest gestures of his hands and murmured sounds of many Afroasiatic dialectic languages, a possible hierarchical linguistic verbal motion structure. Later, becoming Alkebulan, setting an essential foundation for other languages to evolve into different tongues based on inner group/tribal geographical locations. In time, most forgotten is the Godly birthplace of humanity in southeast Afrikus as the limitation of the internal human environment stifled growth and a form of spiritualism ideology inspired deeper into the mindset of a kleptocracy enveloped ruling smaller tribes and nomadic societies that eventually evolved into villages of peoples.

As a character's linguistic verbal structure and early artistic markings evolved into picturesque story writing, man scribed everyday interaction as painted walls and pillars of dwellings and holy temples to be considered God's earthly natural events, many times mythically dressed.

In time, the journeys taken through mortal lives over centuries pleasingly saw humankind settle into their life as individuals with an evolved mind of thought and openly move forward into new areas of inner calmness and spiritual belief.

The curiosity of abundance with natural offerings as a source of survival develops specific knowledge and becomes wise to its use as his fellow man's, creating a greater civilization.

The visit to each century identifying the different theistic ideologies becoming known as religious beliefs became an exciting concept. It provided an insight into the evolution of humanity's acceptance of different idealist concepts of God, as many did and continue to abandon themselves from the original veils of eternal conception. Now forming an amalgamation into organized religion, some truer faiths than others of God's intent. As advocated in most cases, indoctrination by construing scriptures of metaphysical memories and gnostic theistic ideologies became sanitized philosophies of social and political lessons taught by the prophets, disciples, and mentors became the law. If there were any common ground to be found in the centuries with all the religions, it would have to be with the innocent ordinary people being unexposed and those who in earnest spoke and taught the goodness of each day's life that one could live and share with others as a faithful believer in one God, not many gods, and ignored the seeable falsehoods, rather similar to the Essenes in later times. While traveling their journey, many find it more difficult than others to understand the balance between harm and pleasantry, and find themselves in unpredictable circumstances as mortals.

Most make the infallible decision, forgetting the spiritual guide's effort, becoming known as the holy moment in time, praying or meditating for God's guidance.

Some are traveling this mortal journey and come as nonbelievers to see and learn the difference between the faithful and the unendowed or unalienable rights of a true spiritual soul's way through a mortal life. Human life continued its migrations across the great earth in a primitive innocence as other immutable creatures created did so as well and adapted to the ever-changing environment. From the cradle of theology, the East Mediterranean, known as the crescent of harvests, emerged with many faithful teachings and beliefs in monotheistic creator God. Migration of an ideological philosophy evolved into various translated forms of thoughts of the times, losing its foundations of actual truth, which escalated into other established tribal groups and later chieftain states of kleptocracies.

Many lands and island states settled. As we have experienced, the other side of life's hand was the harshness of such teachings misconstrued and forced as the only word of God. If one did not adhere to such indoctrinating religious beliefs, he was subjected to intolerable punishment imposed either by a judgmental society or sought to kill the idolaters thought never to be allowed to enter a promised, discovered heavenly world. The misuse of these ideological, philosophical religions was in the minds of many who developed a more literate intellectualism of domination purposes.

Sometimes, it is a proclaimed cult of sainthoods of egoism amongst all others, and it uses the influence of mythical illusions with organized rhetorical philosophies as indoctrination to the politicization of theistic ideology with the less literate in dominating a civilization.

This stark contrast to the spiritual essence of true believers, who live their lives with the teachings and understanding of wrathfulness and common equity towards their brethren as children of God, is a testament to the misuse of these theistic ideologies. Eventually becoming the ill political practice of wickedness in principalities of power, the darkness of the world. It will remain so for millennia to come as humankind evolves through the coming centuries and millennia. I stand and weep to you as our archangels and great teaching sons of our beloved creator and father. I appeal to the hearts of the genuine, faithful persons who truly comprehend the greatness of God the Almighty.

I urge them, not just as a suggestion but as a call to action, to stand firm and embrace the spiritual essence of true believers, to live their lives with the teachings and understanding of wrathfulness and common equity towards their brethren as children of God. Many do understand their lives as mortal beings. Furthermore, let us delve into the concept of learning lessons with God's guidance. It is about understanding human reasoning, manifesting determined lessons with God's guidance to achieve personal goals, and navigating life's journey without interruptions by other forgetful and unforgiving influences of maliciousness.

The horrid atrocities of inquisitions, tribal warfare, and insidious crusades were carried out as holy wars in the name of God from these misconstrued ideological, theistic philosophies spreading to conquered lands. Subjecting diverse beliefs to claim political kingdoms and territories only to hide behind the shadows of symbols of their mindless falsehoods.

For none of the theistic beliefs were ever the intent nor the holiest of teachings by the great prophets, who had come into a mortal life on behalf of God's will to minister the simplest means of belief in him and learn the veils of life for their journeys.

Very few of humanity knew the reason for his life as a mortal other than survival and the acceptance of rulers' dominant power to be their servants as they were told, and wrongly inserting God's name as a design and cause of strange events. Without their acceptance, one would perish in Tartarus and never be allowed into heaven with God. There is no judgment or guilt from God or man, as there is only the imposed judgment from man to man.

As an angel, I constantly struggled with what I had to endure seeing human society through a millennium in six different centuries. Now, returning to our eternal heavenly dimension with continuous, peaceful, loving life surrounding me, I continued as a high angel to serve our creator, God, and support the archangels' heavenly responsibilities. It is now my position to assist in receiving returning spiritual souls from their mortal journeys into heaven, accompanied by angels, comfort them from their transcending, and assure their healing to begin relieving them of any horrid indoctrinations so imposed upon the mortal character they endured while in the journey.

A cleansing of the spiritual soul and misconstrued implied human influences can take some time, depending on the depth of mental insurgency in the mind of the character portrayed. Eternal life isn't what most indoctrinated populous human species believe it to be, and are led to think using the indifferent ideologies of so-called theistic ministering.

We should conscientiously analyze all issues, gaining knowledge and wisdom, and express such wisdom to others so that they may learn the truths. We all, as angels and archangels, converse many subjects of the past, and that in which we know it shall come and decide which spiritual soul on a journey shall discover such specific knowledge and apply the wisdom to life's methods and philosophies that better the human species in their millennium civilizations while on their journeys. As witnessed through the centuries, wonderful, meaningful philosophers brought the fundamental words of wisdom.

This has always been the allowance through the many centuries of discovery of many subjects, as some are referred to as disciplined natural laws, the four veils of God, and others' encouraging philosophical insights.

All pearls of wisdom can open the real insight into ancient events, thoughts gone or left untrue to mindless false interpretations. As once spoken by an ancient spiritual master, "The lips of knowledge are closed, except to the ears of understanding." I ended my opening talk and thought I truly was in heaven.

I, myself, just a high angel, attend lectures and teachings of our archangels who minister on many subjects by their specific discipline for all of us to learn more of the reasoning of existence from the universe to life and the purpose of evolution through time as the different phases in lifetime itself develop. Sitting upon the holy ground, we all listened to Gabriel, the high archangel, speaking of God's creation of the universe and found it pleasingly interesting and easy for all attending to understand.

Of course, for this reason, we can relay such lectured information to others as necessary in our discussions of life. He first said the universe, as complicated as it seems, is not confusing with a more straightforward explanation of the cause. But, of course, there are endless questions to ask for a purpose that may or may not be explained to us. As he spoke, he stated that the universe is an efficient infinite variable, a cause of unlimited compulsive catastrophic events of expansion of debris, continuous outward unmeasurable dimensional boundaries in the time-space moment to moment.

Moreover, the universe is and never was without elements of a kind, as conditions of immersion of such elements infuse sequences of analogous positive and negative frequencies that occurred by a suggestive cause.

Giving credence to intense debris expulsion into an empty cosmos, gathered forms become known as stars and planets, becoming more defined by extreme centrifugal orbital forces.

The placed planets from the cause of events, some of the significance as other importantly modest remains in a gravitas obliquity orbital sequence to others for a purpose in a measurable time circularity to the universe's central planet of energized forceful light. But! Why the cause? Without created space, without the planets aligned with each other, without the lighted debris continuously expanding through the cosmos, there is no fulfilled universe. In this universe is the Earth with a special species, as that of all created, that survived as perfectly as we like to think, modern humankind, still with a continuous evolutionary process.

Each human species has God's spiritual soul transition as part of creation and functions as the anatomical, biological mass known as the human body. Humankind's created purpose is to be the custodian of the earth for a human's lifespan. Further, humans shall endure an environmental life of the time in which they existed and learn the knowledge of the custodian's purposes for their environment. Each millennium, the human species has evolved through the cycles of time and become known as our Creator's children. Spiritual souls return to a heavenly dimension of eternal life after their mortal lives end. As life is a continuum, there are three primary cycles in the spiritual life. This means there are varying values of the past, present, and future: spiritual life before life (future), life as a spiritual mortal, inner cycles of the time (present), and spiritual life afterlife (past), returning to eternal spiritual life.

There will be several intervals of mortal life for a spiritual soul to live a mortal human life through many evolutionary periods. In the earth's intervals, earlier philosophers were sent to mortal human life to minister such philosophies of creation principles to humanity; many were successful, and others perished. Only basic presumptions were made with limited conscious observations by ancient philosophers with less knowledgeable insight into life's creation to advance beyond the scripted words of texts being ministered through civilizations of ancient and modern millenniums. There is much more to know and accomplish in the eternal dimension, assisting with the returning spiritual souls.

As I helped, many returned. I had met several on my vagabond mortal life journeys and knew their lives as humans and the perseverance with which they lived. The following testimonies of such mortal characters I met and, as a messenger, ministered to our Creator's edicts and principles during their journeys. The Journey of all sons with God in their hearts returns to heaven for Celestia Judicium.

From the testaments, one must recognize and understand the truths of God's edicts and corresponding principles of life he has so orchestrated for mortal human life away from the spiritual soul's eternal life in heaven.

The judgment of mortal human life is not a heavenly commandment, as it has been obliquely imposed for the domination of human civilizations. Therefore, let us reassess God's only commandments for humanity to guide during their mortal journey to please and ease each step taken and lived by daily.

This is all he asked. As an angel, I wonder, thoughtfully, "Is this the mortal life we wish to send our spiritual souls from eternal life to participate in, manifest to learn from, only to return to our dimensional heaven?" Each spiritual soul that journeys is for a reason to participate in any manner to guide civilization itself into the betterment of future living.

An Eternal Life

$\mathcal{E}$ternal life in heaven is exceptional to all holy spirits, for each has the freedom of God's inner gifted will, ministering, and teachings in our Creator's actual beliefs and love. Life is peaceful and loving amongst all his children, sons, and daughters. When teachings are assembled, gatherings with an ability to listen and understand these words of life's guidance to better understand the teachings, the holy Spirit shall transcend to the earthly human life to journey its duration of experiences to understand and implement the teachings in a real-life condition. Not all, if any, occasions are pleasant, and not all are harsh or horrid.

These journeys are continuous throughout an eternal life and may be of many in different times of human evolution through the centuries. God gave human life and allowed such life to evolve through several likenesses, but different in each evolutionary step, with Him creating the earth. God knew the difficulties and pleasantries of human experiences and sent many learned sons and daughters to guide humanity with his loving teachings of philosophies and eternal natural laws to accept and abide by each day of their journey. Knowing not so the case should be, God also knew that with the freedom of conscience and developed cognitive thinking, humans of civilization would establish an organized religion, mostly praising God's four veils of natural laws. In contrast, also knowing the more advanced human mind would be altering the intent to better stand with indoctrination to control the human masses and races, so different as they became a gathered civilization, a standard agenda of political egoism. Further, humanity would migrate to other parts of its created earth, establish different civilizations, and conform to different philosophical faiths in God. From the evolution of migration of humanity, the differences in the evolved interpretations of God's laws and veils could escalate unrest among the faithful and undermine their beliefs. And so, it did and has been upon the earth for millennia of humanity as each declared their scriptures of accurate philosophy were absolute to no other. These differences became known as the atrocities of holy wars, as declared unwarranted faiths continued. Many mortal humans have died because of their ignorance and disobedience of God's veils and principles by adhering to other ideologies, causing the end of a spiritual soul's journey, god manifested for other reasons, only to be ended by egotistical ideological indoctrination.

Even the higher spiritual souls sent by our Creator as his adversaries to guide and minister the veils could not prohibit the ever-continuance of these horrid battles. A spiritual soul's journey in human life can be its hell on earth, greatly influenced by others. The teaching in the eternal heaven is more important to the spiritual souls preparing for the transition to human life's journey and facing such potentially indignant experiences.

The Healings and Teachings

As a high-ranking angel, I am expected to attend healing sessions. Therefore, I assembled teachings of the returning spiritual souls from the mortal human journeys and those elevating closer to an eternal spiritual transition. I rather enjoyed these sessions because I could see the everlasting enthusiasm of each spiritual soul's intent to rid themselves of the inflicted vicious influences of some human's abrasive indoctrinations and subdued controls they may have had to endure. The teachings were mainly conducted by the archangels and higher angels in standing to medium-sized assemblies, so greater attention was given to the individual. The teachings are of the basics of our creator's laws and wishes for the mortal journeys, for each is accompanied by the spiritual guide to influence their inner souls to react or not react in an experience, causing a repercussion of insight to possible greatness or dangers. As the evolution of human life shows, such spiritual guide influences did and did not succeed.

The seven main archangels of great power, protectors, and healers oversee all other angels in ranking and the spiritual souls in eternal life in heaven. The archangels perform divine miracles that align with the souls of angels and spiritual souls by assisting in ascending to a higher plane. Each archangel has its mission of ranking and serving God and his glory, protecting his mystery of spiritual existence in its own dimensional universe.

The individual archangels bring Holy gatherings together to allow complete intuitive attention to the spoken words and meanings of the laws and philosophies so taught and discussed.

Such teaching provides a more in-depth assurance of understanding when a spiritual soul may embark on another mortal life journey and have more acceptance in a mandated experience. Healing a returning spiritual soul after journeying through a mortal life can take time; a mortal life is harsh on many journeys.

On the other side, some mortal journeys are peaceful and less troubling. No one journey is assured of its endurance during a journey, nor the ever-changing environment a mortal life must travel through. Healings are performed thoroughly through a direct inner concentration, spiritual telepathic neural association to cleanse the troubled soul of traumatic events and unpleasant memories of occurrences. The harshest healing and cleansing is to exclude human dimensions of inexplicable injustice that exploit guilt for the denial of accepting human ideology indoctrinations. Through several levels of healing sessions of the telepathic inner association of angels' spiritual souls, cleansings are inevitable for a peaceful, eternal life. Many spiritual souls returned to eternal existence in brutal mental conditions that affected not only their mortal human journey of millions of others through non-spiritual guidance, creating horrid experiences while on earth. These were the longest of healing sessions and asserted levels.

During the mortal journeys, God has only asked the human factor to believe in the four veils and the seven sands of principle life to lead to a better human life in learning the lessons so manifested and enabling enforcement of contributing to the evolution of humanitarian civilizations. As in many returning spiritual souls who endured and experienced harsher occurrences than others, the edicts were sometimes set aside while battling the existence of human life, forgetting how they were established to assist in the presence of mortal life.

Therefore, the Temple of Healing and Teachings is established for assemblies of all returning spiritual souls to reaffirm the affirmations of the Four Veils and Seven Sands of life's principle. But, of course, none of the reaffirmations can be introduced until all healing of the spiritual soul has been cleansed and healed from the mortal life's exploitations and imposed indoctrinations. Therefore, assemblies are kept relatively small in groups for a more concentrated, attentive measure of understanding and ability for personal insight with the archangels. The archangels are the teachers during the assemblies, each of their more qualified and directive responsibilities for assisting with the seven principles of life. The four veils are generally brought forward by angels such as me and others, learning to become faithful teachers in the edicts of God's wishes. Judgment of one's actions as a mortal during their journey is not that of a spiritual nature, as it is an implication of oneself and encouragement through an environmental societal system by humans for dominance over others. Healings are to set free the repercussions of guilt of imposed social judgment by humanity and the spiritual souls' nature of being.

All spiritual souls transcending to a mortal life do so with a purpose of greater integrity aligned with their heart's intuitive wisdom within the manifested character to live. Beyond the four veils and seven sands of life's principles are the spiritual laws of nature and the universe.

These laws are not concerned with absolute or offense while on a mortal journey, but rather with the truth of all, the consequences of their actions and reactions, of an individual spiritual soul.

The Assembly

The Great Hall of Healing and Teaching is a wonderfully peaceful setting for meditative quietness and solemn conversations of learning and hearing the truths of spiritual souls' eternal life and the expressed, endured manifested mortal life of many. An assembly is a small group of spiritual souls who have recently returned from a journey and passed through, receiving immediate inner neural telepathic healings from the greater angels of life, the healers. The spiritual souls are assessed for their depth of needed healing, for most are shorter than others, while some must continue into healing for some time. Attendees comfortably sat on the rugs and pillows on the floor while the speaker(s) sat in an armchair, the humanitarian art of the millennium decorating the surroundings.

Many spiritual souls gathered and placed themselves in a restful, relaxed position, quietly chatting with others while the assembly was coming together. Then, as a high angel, I walked in, sat in the soft chair, and waved my hand and arm in a circular motion to gather the attendees' attention and bring the session to harmony.

I spoke in a soft orating voice, welcoming everyone and assuring them we were pleased with their triumphant return to eternal happiness in heaven. As I now had control and everyone's attention.

"Please allow me to introduce myself to each of you, for some of you may already know me; I am Elijah, the high angel to the archangel council, and I am here to begin this assembly as part of the healing process upon your return from your mortal life journey. Since humanity's existence on God's earth, I have been on several mortal human journeys. Some of you may not recognize me as I do you during one or more of your journeys."

The room was quiet as everyone listened to my words, and I continued. "I wish to start with the assurance that the eternal dimension is not a magistrate nor a place of decisions for one's contemporary mortal life, and there is no such mystic ideology called judgment. Judgments are human social institutions to provoke an imposed guilt for an acceptance of an ideological indoctrination upon an individual or society for domination."

One may impose guilt upon themselves because of their existing environment for a cause." They all looked at each other and listened. I said, " The assembly sessions are all part of the healing process upon your return from the mortal journey endured, to bring to light the truth of your manifested actions living through the journey, and to understand the consequences of an experience you faced as a lesson in life. Not for imposed guilt by others." I went on further, stating. "We shall review the Four Veils our creator placed forward to us all in acceptance and dwell during the journey. We shall also review the Seven Sands of life's principles given by each archangel responsible for encouraging the principle understandings." Again, the spiritual souls turned to each other in whispers of curiosity and a look of wonder. I smiled and said.

"I know you may feel somewhat confused, but also know some of you lived this journey well in understanding its meaning, or close thereof, and performed your lives to the best you could with the four veils of God and seven principles of spiritual laws. Some may have done so unknowingly of the awareness of action." I stopped for a minute, then said. "I realize in many of your mortal human lives, you did not understand the purpose of the character life you lived. In its simplicity, look backward to the section of a decade you lived in and try to understand the life of that time, then move forward into the next phase, and so on. You will then understand more clearly what and why your manifested journey was about."

I looked out for each other as I made eye contact, seeing the goodness in their hearts. "I may even call upon one or two of you concerning an experience and a lesson learned from what you may have encountered. But first, let me reiterate the importance that the assemblies are not a call for the judgment of your mortal life actions, but only a consideration of the consequences of the actions you endured and their reasonable applicability to the spiritual laws of life.

We here know many of you were forced into human civilization's impulses of actions and performed differently from God's manifested wishes. We understand and are here to heal the spiritual soul of these impositions. Further, the goodness and or greatness of these laws you were able to ensure bring to your environment of mortal life, commonly known as a spiritual moment."

You could feel the room become more peaceful and less restless, and smiles of happiness prevailed as they spoke softly to each other again. We all know God, our Father, creator of ALL, did so with the most excellent care and intention for a new universe of planets, with only one having the environmental ability to sustain created life.

However, the idea of humanity is only indeed known to our Creator as he has chosen through the evolutional variations of humanity's indifferences to each other into the human social, homo erectus species of today and the future. For each evolution, man has evolved and developed his intellect and physical appearance for a reason: adapting to an ever-changing planet with its living matter. Therefore, God created the spiritual soul, such as yourselves, in his image and likeness and made a human species from the elements of the living environment of his planet, named Earth. From this human species created, there are two of one kind, male and female, for the purpose, as that of all living creatures on earth. For they, as you being spiritual souls, shall multiply into many by their means and God's will.

Therefore, there are two different worlds in two different dimensions. The world where we all live as angels, archangels, and spiritual souls with God our Father is an eternal heavenly world for life. On the other hand, the earthly dimension of humanity is a journey lived in sessions of time, with a beginning and an ending. As many of you have already experienced and understood, as spiritual souls, you must transcend to the earthly dimension, a spiritual soul into a human's evolving development, giving a human its life and being born through birthing nurturers.

The new human birth will become one of the physical characteristics of both nurturers. They will experience life to learn lessons of humanity and evolve into characters that will contribute to the development of human society's civilizations, no matter the pleasantries or unpleasantness.

This is known as Life before Life, Life in Life, and Life after death. These journeys shall be made more than once as a spiritual soul, only each time to return home to eternal life with our Creator. I looked over the small group again and was assured of their attention following our talk and explaining essential points to remember during our sessions. I said. "Now, we all reside here in this beautiful temple of Healing to learn more about your journey through reviewing the Four Veils and Seven Sands of life's principles."

I must first inform you of what we here in our heavenly dimension have contributed to humanity and the millennia of civilizations through time. As spiritual souls, each of you journeyed for more than one reason to learn and experience humanity's culture and be teachers and scholars of understanding to society.

Many of you were characterized as a justification to evolve with gained knowledge and thought with great wisdom, leaving humanity with answers they may acquire and utilize to develop into more excellent societies." I could see on their faces bewilderment when only a few smiled in acceptance, in understanding the mortal life they had left. The least they knew was the justification for using them in the living human character; they were suitable or justifiable to be what they were to perform and leave humanity with. The heavens provided transcending souls to mortal human life with ideas and clues to the secrets of life, some with numeric conditions and philosophies to better society, only to have them named mystic passages of a dreamed hellion of malevolence. An intention of character, even here in the spiritual world, seemed to forget that human nature can be influenced by environmental conditions, leading to egoism for indoctrination and domination of the other, of the simplest-minded humans. We have certainly learned that such actions, in many cases, must be repeated more than once through the millennia of human civilizations, for in each evolution of humanity, the act and reaction of experiences seem to revolve around the cause of misunderstanding of God's Veils and Principles for a better society. However, others performed well in the most straightforward manner and succeeded in the greater interest of humanity, leaving benefactors of ancient papyrus-scripted scrolls to guide humanity throughout history. Most were acceptable with reason, and others were reputable with definitely slanted truths for indoctrination and dominance over a free spiritual soul in human character.

I looked again at the group and could see I still had their full attention, and their interest was greater as they chatted. I held up my arm, giving a sign of attention, please. Then, as they all looked up, I said. "I shall tell you stories of several God's sons, his children as you, who returned from their mortal journeys and were healed as you are being, and only to be told of their return very soon as a different character in a new century for more experiences of humanity." I continued. "For the new characters of each shall be historically entwined in different times of civilizations."

As I began telling the stories of different spiritual souls, each with different manifested mortal lives, they looked with wonder and intrigued curiosity.

THE FIRST STORY

◆———————————————————◆

Returning Home,
My Son Spiritual Soul of Christianity

ריס טיאן הבן את העברית

Beloved Immanuel (Yeshua) receiving John.

The Return, My Son, The Christian Spiritual Soul

A quiet breeze moves over Golgotha as the clouds darken the day's sun into the night. All of life is still in a nervous silence on earth this day...
And for the many millennia to come...in remembrance
My son...lowered from the cross of crucifixion...
by James and his mother Mary and (Ishanh), lay wrapped in a blood-covered shroud....in a lifeless natal cradle in his mother's arms... the last moment of a loving passion as she wept... and she wept.

The angels sang out in a heavenly chorus,

"Oh, be that of life received: this our son in heaven."

As it was my tears from the peaceful streams..., I washed his loving face of sorrows and cleansed the sins of our believers...those who believe in me as we...now exalted and with forgiveness...to all.

"For theists know not what they do."

Upon this, the third day so passed in time...

shall always be the day my son, "The Christian," known throughout the lands as Jemanual, left such a brutal but peaceful mortal life of teaching.

The truths of one's wisdom of the four veils to their spiritual souls, only to show his mortal faith in meeting the disciples with blessings....For he never came home to me to be as we...in the kingdom of our heaven.

Part I

The Beloved John, Brother of Immanuel (Yeshua)

And John said to me. 'You are the vagabond I saw yesterday on the hill, sitting and watching us walk past, taking Immanuel, my brother's body, to the cave, and you made a very distinct sign with your hand as we passed. It was similar in shape to a cross as you moved your hand up and down and across your chest. I looked at him and said. "Yes, that is a sign of a cross you saw me make in honor and peace of Immanuel upon the wooden cross on which he died." He looked at me again and said. "How is it you know him?" I said Immanuel is a well-known prophet and life teacher ministering God's words." We walked away from the crowd and sat at an outside tavern table as he requested that refreshments be brought to us, and we drank fresh pomegranate juice. He asked me more questions about how I knew of Immanuel and his teachings, being a vagabond. He asked. "What do you call yourself?" I said. "My name is Elijah Malachi."

He looked at me and said. " In Hebrew, that means God's messenger, correct?" "Yes," I replied. I looked at him and said. "You must be John the apostle and a disciple of Immanuel who has walked with him to teach and minister such words of God and ease the way for him to gather others to listen?" Suddenly, he sat back and looked at me very seriously and said. 'Who are you, vagabond, just who are you, and why are you here knowing me and all of Immanuel, our teacher of God's way?'

I looked back at him with a smile and said. "First, I know why you are the only disciple to be with Immanuel and witness the horrible atrocity of the crucifixion, and the others were not present to pray for him and ask God's relief from his pains?" He hung his head and said the others fled, for they were afraid for their lives, having been associated with Immanuel and feared they would be crucified or executed in a horrible manner as Immanuel. "On the other hand, I believe so much in him that I could not stay away and not be there to comfort his mother, Mary, and friends the best I could," I responded. "I am a messenger; " I know all, and you should listen, for we have more to discuss, for you to learn and understand the future in God's teaching by his word. For this is your journey ever so planned in heaven before you were born into this mortal life you live. God asked you to return from the spiritual soul to mortal human life from his kingdom to be part of Immanuel's life as he ministers humankind with the truth of God's will for all during their journeys to learn and understand the righteous of life, for one day all shall return to the Kingdom to live eternally."

I continued to say and explain. "Your Journey shall be to inscribe the ministering words of Immanuel for the future in the millennia to come to know his words of human peace. I continued. "You shall bring integrity, knowledge, the wisdom of God's words, trust of faith to nature's edicts, and sensitivity of acceptance in the principles and wonders of God's spiritual inner created gifts. Your journey has only just begun, for you shall always enjoy the pleasure of abundance in knowledge and nature's foods of wealth as your worth."

I further explained. "With this abundance is the power bestowed upon you to deliver the faithful truth of God's humanitarian wishes for life." I knew then that John knew his journey's purpose to endure; I was well into my century task of meeting him with a message and spiritual guidance. Almost 280 years later, after the crucifixion of Immanuel, he came to be known as Jesus Christ from the Greek title words Jesus the anointed one and the word Christo, prince of peace, ιησούς Χριστός. John and James alike became disciples and traveled the lands ministering the edicts and Veils' philosophical words of God, as that of Immanuel, a simple man, bringing loving peace to all with healing lyrics to the ill. In particular, having learned to read and write in Greek, John inscribed many verses and words from memory, all that he and others following Immanuel could remember. The most vibrant message to say all human life is God's children, the sons and daughters. Sketched on the earliest of paper, papyrus, an Egyptian development from centuries past, kept such ministries of God's will and veils safe for the future. John and James faced the adversaries of Roman territorial prosecutions and martyrdom as they were arrested, and John even survived being boiled in water and death. Finally, John was delivered from death and sentenced to the mines in prison on the Island of Patmos. While in prison in Patmos, John, the beloved disciple and apostle, wrote the first scripted philosophies of the Book of Revelation, to be later included in a book known as the Holy Bible, which would be re-scripted many times through the centuries of found religion, Christianity. The only dissatisfaction throughout the millennia was that many versions were written to distort the truth for hegemonic human dominance. Years later, John was freed and returned to serve as the Bishop of Edessa in Turkey.

Mid-spring, in the small foothills of the Turkish countryside, was always swept with cooling breezes of fresh cider scents from the nearby forests. John lay quietly upon his bedding, knowing the journey of mortal life was nearing its end. He remembered many earlier days in Judia countryside, walking with Immanuel as the youngest disciple, ministering God's words of a peaceful, loving life without guilt. Staring at the ceiling and then glancing through the open window at the approaching evening and his friends and loved ones standing by his side, John could see in his own eyes a brightness of flicking images and knew they were angels overseeing his final hours. He turned and glanced back at his family with a smile of thankfulness and glee in his eyes with praise them for their support throughout his journey. He had seen more than others would ever know or understand the pain he felt when Immanuel, a simple, loving man (to become titled Jesus Christ), was crucified on that day in Jerusalem. But too, the wonderous, peaceful love he felt when blessing and baptizing others into the faith of God as the only God. John's mortal body slowly became numb as it started closing and stopping functioning, and his eyes slowly closed to the mortal light of life. At that exact moment, the angels reached out to his spiritual soul. The angels raised his spiritual soul from the mortal body to transcend into the dimensional heavens to return to the Kingdom of heaven of eternal spiritual love. James died as an older man and was the only apostle to die peacefully, approximately 80 A.D.

Part II

A Vagabond's Return Home

I was peacefully sitting on the veranda in one of my favorite places in Heaven and closing my eyes to imagine the spiritual breezes cooling my face and smelling the wonderful scent of flowers from the gardens below.

I, Elijah, a high angel in eternal life, had more time for peacefulness because of all the transcending mortal lives I had lived and learned to minister to the many younger angels and bring healing to them who had returned from the guide of their mortal journey many who for the first time shall transcend into the mortal world to journey. I was always involved with the archangels in deciding who and why an angel should transcend and experience a mortal life, and what lessons in that life need to be shared and learned. At times, it was challenging to make such decisions because we who had experienced such matters in a mortal life knew either the difficulty or peacefulness of the energy the angel would live. I had transcended many times on short trips to meet the angels in their mortal life to provide support and guidance, and hopefully preserve them on the path

God and the archangels intended for their journey. Unfortunately, mortal life journeys are not as easy and peaceful as one may think or imagine, for sometimes harsh lessons and experiences must be experienced. The last trip I was assigned led me to six different centuries over one thousand years to meet people of diverse backgrounds and cultures with different faiths and beliefs in God.

Some had ministered falsehoods, thinking a single innovative scripture of a religious concept, as it became a social interaction of others being imbued with such ministering for domination, imposing guilt. The extended journey was a wonderful, pleasing experience, and reporting the archangels and God our Father's findings brought immense pleasure to me as a senior angel. As I sat quietly in a meditative moment of peace, it was suddenly interrupted by a young serving angel reaching over to touch my shoulder and wake me. I opened my eyes and turned to ask why I was being disturbed. The young angel server said. " Senior Angel, there is a request for you to come as soon as possible to the Healing Temple and meet a new returning spiritual soul who keeps asking for you," I asked. "And who is that asking for me?" He replied, "I am not sure, sire, but they said it was urgent for your needed presents." I stood and gathered myself and thanked the young angel for delivering the message, and I began my walk to the Temple of Healing, where all transcending spiritual souls come upon their return from mortal life journeys. The Temple of Healing is divided into several sections depending on the condition of the returning spiritual soul. Mortal life can be ruthless through the centuries of human cultural civilizations, leaving the returning spiritual soul in mental despair and requiring prolonged healing.

After a short walk through the heavenly gardens, I reached the temple's steps and entered the great hall of section one, the receiving rooms. I was met by another serving angel who led me through the crowded space of new returnees.

Sitting in a corner was a spiritual soul figure resembling the characteristics of John the Disciple, now better known by the Christian mortals as the Beloved Apostle by all he ministered. John turned and saw me coming, jumped to his feet with a great smile, wrapped his arms around me, and cried. "Thank God, Elijah, you are here. I feel safe knowing you were right when we met the day after the crucifixion of Immanuel. Can I see him?" I smiled and said. "No, not yet; you must remain here in the Temple of Healing for some time to be spiritually restored and relieved of all that may have unknowingly harmed your spiritual soul while enduring the infectious atrocities in your mortal journey. For we know most of it was not easy for you." I said to him with a blessing, "You shall see all in time, but first, you are safe now at home for your eternal life to join us." I knew he was close to Immanuel, now historically known as Jesus Christ; Yeshua, we spoke of him in heaven and wanted to renew his loving friendship accordingly. Sooner than he knows, which will make him happy, we all listen well to God's great teachers and prophets.

I told John that as his healing process began, I, too, would listen to his experiences endured as the healing process is not or never shall be a judgment of one's mortal journey as it is learning of their experiences in genuinely understanding for themselves the needed lessons of life while even teaching humanity of God's words and veils to better live through a mortal life. His journey was to accompany his brother Immanuel, a simple man of the times as a jew who learned the Hebrew ways and had earlier traveled to other lands and learned of human-minded peace of the eastern world and how to accept the truths of God's humanity life upon his earth. Several days had passed when again I was summoned to visit the Temple of Healing to hear more human life experiences. Many were loving and wonderful heart-filling moments, and many horrific times imposed upon a human soul, apparently barbaric, upsetting the course of one's journey.

In such matters, remarkable healings are needed to ensure the spiritual soul is well and peaceful in our heavenly dimension, and eternal life with us all as angels is a most peaceful, loving life. As receiving angels, we are not here to judge one action in response to an experience, no matter its difficulty, adversity, or pleasantry. We are here to learn of the incident from an assigned learning view. Did mortal life learn from the experience? Had human life completed the trusted manifested life? I saw John sitting off in the distance, wrapped in a warm cloth and a distance look of meditation as he blankly stared into the heavens.

I slowly approached him, knelt beside him, and reached to touch his arm in a loving, peaceful way, with a smile as I asked. "Beloved brethren, how do you feel today?" He smiled as he replied. "I feel for the first time in many years of enduring the mortal life so much at peace in my heart. But remain unsure of my judgment for the life I lived and if I accomplished every lesson I was born to learn while living that life?" I stood, pulled near a soft bench, and held his arm gently and lovingly. I smiled back with encouraging eyes of assurance and said. "My brother, I must first enlighten you with wonderful news and great assurance that there is no judgment of your life experiences, for you lived a magnificent life as a follower and teacher with Immanuel, who was always referred to as Yeshua and centuries later given the title Jesus Christ as the newly forming Christian theology was forming by others. You were one of the first worthy followers and guided humanity in establishing a great faith in his honor. Only later did such ministering become a religion of the world throughout many civilizations. This was manifested as part of your mortal life, and you did so superbly against difficult adversities in backward, uncivilized circumstances. Further, you inscribed the writings of his great ministry to all humanity and those in need of his faith to believe in God our Father." I rested a moment as I continued. "The inscribed book of your so-called Revelations gives great guidance to all, even though it may not be as accurate as considered, but attentive to the true words of God in many respects, but unfortunately rewritten many times to ensemble a civilization's hegemonic agendas society. Nevertheless, it serves humanity and true believers a great purpose". He smiled at me and said thank you for your confidence. I did say in addition. "For you are home now in eternal life and shall hear the real truth of God about what all has been ministered in confidence by many great teachers and prophets of God has sent to live mortal lives as you did." "It is not the place for us here in eternal life to judge you, but praise you for the peacefulness, acceptance of wisdom you brought to humanity while enduring pleasantries, but then again, terrible atrocities imposed upon you by the ills of humanity. You have left a memory and an astounding mark in history, never to be forgotten for centuries to come." I stopped for a minute to breathe with him in peace, and then said.

"Do you remember the day we met in the streets of Jerusalem, we talked, and I told you I was a messenger of God, and then you graciously invited me into your home? You opened your heart and home to me. It was a spiritual moment placed upon you. You, James, Mother Mary, and Magdalena listened to the true words of God's wishes for humanity, and now you have lived those wishes in truth and the visions of righteousness in the four veils and seven principles with spiritual laws."

"So, bless you, my brother, for now; you shall heal and later join us all and sit beside us in guidance to others leaving for their mortal journey. The great words inscribed will prevail for you to sit beside us all to guide others in the stability of integrity and wisdom." Finally, one day of heavenly time, John sat down with Immanuel, who had become known as Jesus by mortal humanity, renewed their beloved brotherhood, and remained close throughout eternity. I rose from sitting and smiled as I walked away, leaving John with pleasant tears, a gleaming smile, and a more loving feeling of a guiltless heart. For now, he shall spend time healing with our angels and recovering from the mortal life he had to live. I knew I would be returning in the days to come and listening to the healings of his journey. One day in heavenly time, he shall journey again as a newly manifested human character. I saw so many others this day who had arrived in their spiritual soul returning from the mortal lives they had lived, wondering of all their stories and if all had experienced the lessons to learn from and how many returning had their journeys cut short because of human brutality inflicted upon them because of unjust civilizations laws.

The faces I could see almost told such stories of each, many old in appearance but happy, and others young with saddened reflections of being lost in wonder, as angels gathered to assist them in peace. All are at home in eternal life and shall be healed with God's blessings. In days to come, Elijah, a high heavenly Angel, will always be next to the arch angels, respectfully answering to God and listening to the Sons of God, the prophets, and teachers who knew the truths of life and heaven for all.

I was always involved in providing my opinions using mortal life experiences and usefully seeing the experiences considered for others to leave on a new mortal journey. I was always asked to support the Temple of Healing in receiving the returning spiritual souls from their mortal journeys. Always listening to the returning spiritual soul's stories of how they were influenced and coerced into accepting a religion with beliefs, and to feel the guilt of nonacceptance is denied.

For we in the eternal life all knew from when the great prophets and teachers returned from their journeys in teaching and ministering God's word and veils of life, the custodians and others used these verses and prophecies to control the masses of civilizations for egotistical power and control of territories. The effects of indoctrination to dominate worked well through the centuries and inconceivably disregarded human life because one believes in God, if not adhering to their own belief. However, I did return to sit in on discussions the healing angels were having with John and listened to his remarks regarding the scripture he wrote called Revelations, particularly on what he had conceived as judgment.

The healing angels said they knew of mortal life's explanation for humans being forced to have civilizations live more peacefully in order. Using a marked act as a sin gave culture the false right to impose guilt of execution upon those who did not obey. As backward and, in many cases, humankind developed in purity as angels' sins became human nature and caused corruption with deceit and insatiable ambitions. The judgment was set in place by humanity, not heaven. All human acts were, in some cases, horrific but also an experience of learning, except for those who committed genocide against the human race. It is the place of the healing angels to pursue and induce spiritual healings to heal the horrid of a returning pious spiritual soul, no matter how difficult it may be and the length of time to bring the spiritual soul back to God's will. From the moment of spiritual healing, life becomes an eternity in the heavenly dimension with God and all the brethren's angels and spiritual souls. Nonbelievers are also healed from their mortal life as nonbelievers to learn the difference between true beliefs and having to endure a mortal life as a nonbeliever. For all, they had gone to mortal life to be a particular character in an environment to live for a reason, only to return to be healed of all that was endured in their mortal life. For now, understanding the designed purpose of his true mortal life as Jesus's brother having an abundance and power to minister Jesus's words of God and prophies, he knows his life was rewarding.

"Heal and Restore their souls, for God's Children have returned home."

THE SECOND STORY

Returning Home,

My Son Spiritual Soul, the Newest Believer

MEA FILIUS IN NEMO FIDELIS

"Take this, my spiritual soul, to the eternal dwelling of thy Father."

MEA FILIUS IN NEMO FIDELIS

A lost generation of infinite light... the knowledge of faith,
Fall not away... or shade thy self of shame from my likeness...
Nor feel frightened with despair...I am not hidden from the generations.
Your conscious compassions have failed with the loss of faith in me.
Misguidance of truths for justice and mercy has become an Imbalance and immoral ritual that disrupts life's peaceful rhythms in the universe within you.
A soul becoming lost to a world of nowhere....

My son of such nonbelief...lay down your shield.
And fold back the mystic curtain...of heretic satanic vices
That underlies your quivered foundation.
And a broken sword of harmony to life
Kneel and bow thyself before me for a blessing to
Stand forth and accept me and build a faith belief in me...
Ascend to the four veils of life to be.
For with this hand... I give you a new spiritual belief.
Of the divine immanence of me...

"Thy will be done."

Your strengthened soul of being...an infinite rewarding faith in me.
For I am higher than all I created in this...
My universe with dominion overall. `
For all shall be forgiven....is forgiven...

Part I

~~~

My Son Septimus, the Gladiator, A Believer

A t the beginning of the third century A.D., Constantius was the Augustus of the western territories, Severus was the Caesar, and Galerius was the Augustus of the eastern regions. Constantine was the son of Constantius, who was dying, and his troops named Constantine the new Augustus. Using the battle of Milvian and Victor, Constantine forms an Alliance with Licinius in the east. The new world of Christianity came together after Constantine admitted to a vision of a cross in the sky and fell to their admission and faith to become a Christian, forming the new ruling government in Rome as a Christian-based foundation of the new country. Even Constantine's sister became Christian. The executions and prosecutions of Christians stopped in the amphitheaters. The Roman citizens would have religious freedom to whomever they chose without trouble from the empire. Although this did not mark Christianity as an official religion of the kingdom, those who chose could still follow paganism. This created somewhat of a religious cold war because Licinius and the Greeks disagreed with monotheism and tried to overpower and influence paganism. Others stared at me like they recognized that I was not a local citizen and was a vagabond in nature. I realized I was hungry and had not eaten anything in some time.

I stepped out of the fountain water and looked around for a food vendor to whom I could offer my services for a piece of bread and drink. None were in the plaza, but I saw a cart with bread down one alleyway.

I walked in that direction when I was knocked to the cobblestone very harshly, hitting my head and dropping my staff. I lay dazzled on the ground for a minute when this strong-handed man reached for me, picked me up with one hand and arm, and tried to stand me upright, handing me my staff to balance myself. I was still mindless in thought as to what had happened. This immense structure of a man smiled at me and apologized for accidentally knocking me to the ground, and asked if I was okay. I responded. I am not sure as yet. I am older, and gathering myself takes me a minute." He was so apologetic and sorry for his actions, as he said. "Please, my citizen friend, let me acquire a refreshing drink to help you feel better." I looked at him and said. " Bless you, my son. That would be gratefully accepted." He looked stunned momentarily by my speech and the words I used to thank him. He said. "Who are you? You are not Roman and not a citizen, are you?" I replied. 'No, I am called Elijah Malachi, known as the messenger of God." My Latin was still coming into focus to correct speaking dialect with a slight accent, not being a Roman. He smiled and said. "Come, my friend, let us drink a refreshing drink and toast life, for you are unharmed and safe now." I followed him at an alarming pace; he was so big and robust in structure, dressed in a high clothe tunic with a gold border, and with a red cloth robe thrown across his broad shoulders and held one end over his right arm and I managed to keep up as he leads me to a corner stall near the plaza. We sat on a bench at a table as he told the waiting proprietor to bring a drink and bread. He asked. "You said you were a messenger of God?" Which one of these crazy monstrous idols did you come from to bring a message to, and to what citizens are seeking with this message?"

I took a minute as I broke my bread with a slight prayer of thanks, ate my first bite, and said. "I come only with one God, the creator of all things and mankind, for there is no other God or Gods in the universe as he." He looked at me and said. I do not believe in these Gods and statues and their prophecies of life and lies of my fellow man. I said. 'That is good, for there is no other but one God who is here for you and sent you to live this life's journey." He barked back at me as I ate and drank in hunger. "Do you know who I am and how important I am here in this city as a citizen? "No," I said. He said. "I am Septimus, the great gladiator of all time. I have fought many battles in my Emperor's Coliseum, defeating all my enemies and beasts who came out to destroy me in life." I looked at him and said. "You are the seventh child in your family of the sixth son, your father born in 285 A.D. "Yes, I know." He said as he looked stunned and again remarked. "How is it you know this, and did you know he is not my father of birth, nor his wife my mother? I was left as a newborn babe in the streets wrapped in a cloth to die when a man, my father, picked me up and raised me as the man I am today." I smiled, nodded, and said. " I know some of you, your discipline of greatness, your integrity and favored citizenship in Roma, and your disbelief in all the false Gods scattered around the city to be praised in untrue strengths and unworthiness to protect you." We sat, ate, and drank, as I could see he would have many questions for me to try and answer. He looked at me and said.

"So! This one God you speak of can do all that the many other Roman and Greek gods can do?" I replied, "Yes, and more. He is the only God and creator of all things, including you.

He has put you on this life's journey in which you live and have succeeded as a great gladiator, a very disciplined man seeking freedom, and now a free man because of your wisdom and integrity. God believes and loves you for the person you are and all you do for humankind and shall carry forth the rest of your life with such wisdom to teach and love others for their human being and the journey they must endure." He looked puzzled again and said. "Are you one of these persons that our new Emperor Constantine is calling the Christians, we as citizens are supposed to start believing in and live a more peaceful life?" I replied. "God is the same in which they believe, and I also believe and follow each day, and pray for life's guidance. No, I am not a Christian or of any religion, for I am an angel of faith on a journey through your century, as I said, a messenger of God for God's service to humanity." I knew that Septimus did not see the reason and purpose for his mortal journey through this life. After a long visit of many days with moments of talking about our God and his acceptance in their life's journey, I left Septimus and his family to go forward in their new world of belief to live in the best peacefulness possible and behold life's integrity true to all humanity. I knew my purpose for this journey was complete.

I waited for several hours for everyone to retreat to their quarters and chambers, then climbed the stairs to the villa's rooftop, where I found a private patio area and lay to rest in the cool night air.

As I was falling asleep, I prayed to God to accept my journey's success. I was ready to leave this century and return home with his blessings. I fell into a deep, unconscious slumber, not finishing my prayer request.

Part II

The Vagabond's Return Home

In Heaven, I was very busy at the Temple of Healing, working with newly arriving spiritual souls returning from their mortal life journey. I comforted them as each became aware they were spiritually alive in a new dimensional world called the Kingdom of Heaven. Many were unsure and afraid of where they were, but all were graciously cared for and loved by our angels. This day was more crowded than most, and many new spiritual souls kept arriving with their guiding angels.

Some with familiar family and friends already had angels supporting them as they stepped into the new world. We rarely see so many come unless it's a day when humanity is culturally or theologically in a state of opposition and warring, causing the end journeys of many mortal lives, leaving their mortal bodies to decay with ignorant, egotistical honors and their spiritual souls to return to heaven. In many cases of this nature, ending a human journey in an untimely manner will require the spiritual soul to return to its revived human character or another unborn mortal body at some other time and complete its originally designed journey accordingly. The designated time of the end of life set to transcend home was not to be at that particular moment of the journey.

Through the centuries and more so in modern humanity, this is becoming more acknowledged as a miss transcendent, being referred to as a near-death experience. Sometimes coordinated by angels to assure the spiritual soul on the human journey that all is well, or corrections in the journey need to be made. Testaments to this are the stories told to others of the out-of-body experience.

As I watched the new arrivals in the background, I noticed a spiritual soul figure of a substantially older man, a Roman tunic and robe of distinction, assisted by guardian angels, entering the receiving area. I stared momentarily and recognized him as Septimus, the Roman gladiator I had visited on one of my remarkable journeys. He looked old and weak from an arduous mortal life journey. I knew of the difficulties he had endured as a gladiator to gain his freedom to become a citizen of the Roman Empire. I knew in his free life how he accepted God as his only God and sought to encourage others to learn more and accept the newly organized religion of Christianity after years of publicly executing them in the coliseum, representing Roman victory war games. I walked over and smiled as he stood momentarily and stared at me with wonder, trying to place me. I spoke up with a smile. "Septimus, it is me, Elijah, the vagabond who visited you many years ago and stayed with you and your family, learning about God's truth and your acceptance to follow Christianity instead of another religious philosophy." He looked again and stared with the most significant curiosity, for he could not recognize me dressed as an angel, not an old, ragged vagabond man.

Suddenly, a smile appeared on his face, his eyes gleamed with sparkle, and a tear appeared as he reached out to hug me. He said. " Oh, dear God, thank you for being here for me. I am so lost and unsure of where I am. I thought I would be in Hades, facing the devil after the terrible things I did to humanity, and pay harshly for my sins."

He fell to his knees, grabbed my hands, and cried, asking for forgiveness. I reached out and lightly stroked his head and said. "Have nothing to fear, my brethren; you are in a life of eternity with all of us and safe, never to fear the evil horridness of mortal life coming ever again." I motioned him to stand and to follow me to a quieter place to talk. The other angels departed to leave us to talk. I wanted to ease Septimus's feelings and assure him he was safe from any indoctrinated belief of judgment and the non-existence of a place called the underworld, so brainwashed and endorsed by mortal humanity to ensure egotistical dominance over cultural civilizations. I assured Septimus that he did many great things in his journey to create a heavenly love while on earth. I motioned for Septimus to sit, relax, and breathe the new heavenly air so clear and different from Earth's mortal environment. After transcending, I turn and motion for a serving angel to bring a drink to quench my thirst. He smiled comfortably and felt more relaxed now, knowing where he was and safe with a teacher he had learned from in the past.

I looked at him with a smile and said. Septimus, it's been a long time since we saw each other, and we enjoyed our visit years ago. How is the family, and how was life after I left?"

He stared into the cosmos for a moment, smiled, and said. "After you came and visited and showed us all and explained many things to my family about God and the teachings of his son

Immanuel, as you had explained, now we call him Jesus Christ. How we should accept and believe in the Four Veils of the Seven Sands of spiritual guidance, providing truthful guidance to live as mortals and our journey's purpose, we led a wonderful, loving life." He continued." We shared as much as we could with all we greeted. My wife and I believed in sharing our fortune with those less fortunate." He hesitated a minute and said. "But only attending the meetings when I could, my wife devoted herself to attending several times a week and became very vocal about her belief. One day, she became even more belligerent and said she was possessed by a "ruah" (demonic spirit). My family, son, daughter, and the servants were scared of her, and she stayed locked in a room alone." I asked. "What did you do"? He looked at me with sad, almost broken eyes of tears and said. " I talked to the priest at her temple of worshiping, and he said she was being possessed either by the old Roman Gods myths in polytheism or by the old Hebrew demons, and he would send a holy practitioner to work with her as what was known as an exorcism in nature to expel such "ruah" demons and return her mental being become more Christ-like in her life, an absolute believer." I thought about what he said and very quietly, in a soft voice, said to him.

"Septimus, one very important thing you must remember when someone in a mortal life seems to think they are possessed. First, a person like your wife is not regarded as evil or responsible for their actions and deceitful words. They are victims of extreme, insidious theistic humanitarian indoctrination and manipulation by others for egoism and purposes used for hegemonic political control, making others feel guilty for not believing as they are told and further told the demons of the past shall devour their souls." He looked at me momentarily and said, "You mean all the guilt I, too, had as well,

I felt for not being able to help her was based on others' manipulation for their betterment"? I shook my head yes. I said. "Fear not, my brother, when she passes and transcends here to heaven, we will work with her as we have done for millenniums with many of our returning spiritual souls to heal them from the mental atrocities of human indoctrination on many different manners endured from civilization for she has God within her, same as you." He looked at me again with a smile and a moment of relieving peacefulness. I asked. "Whatever happened to the crippled boy, an orphan, who opened the gates for us that morning at the coliseum?" Septimus smiled and said. " I helped him by finding him a more meaningful position with an active gladiator, being his page, cleaning and caring for his equipment for fighting." As he gleamed with pride for his work, he also said. "I also helped him to sit and learn to read Latin and some Greek by a teacher in his off time, and he has done well since." I smiled and shook my head in approval of his support.

Septimus was curious in a troubling way and expressed such on his face and turned, looked around at others in the area, and then said. "Am I here to be judged by God for all the wrongs I committed to other mortal beings and many other erroneous life matters? Please forgive me."

Lowering his head in shame, he popped up and said. "If I must go to this place called Hades as told I would for such misgivings, then so be it. I tried to do my best once I accepted God as my only salvation and helped others to believe." I stared at him for a minute with sorrow, knowing he truly had been misled by the powerful use of religion to indoctrinate the citizenship and his mortal life journey, and the ordered killing of others, shortening their journeys, taking their future away from them. But also knew how he was awarded his freedom and became a Christian, accepting God our Father and Creator as the only God of all things. I placed my hand on his large shoulders and said. "No, you are not here to be judged for what inhumane behavior you were ordered to perform for survival by the insidious civilizations of backward unknowing peoples, nor be sent to your mythical indoctrinated place called Hades, the non-existing underworld." He looked at me even more curiously, stunned. I stared into his eyes to let him know I was being truthful. "You are returning from a long mortal journey that was planned for you many years ago for you to endure the pains and misgivings of having to do as you did for survival by disciplining yourself to earn first your freedom from the shackles of backward political egotistical humanity and then learn many lessons from these experiences as you certainly have proven. You were expected to do everything you did and even more, as instructed by the evilness of egotistical humans seeking and holding hegemonic power of guilt over you to gain your freedom." He just sat there listening.

I continued. "I came to visit you as requested by God and guided by the archangels at that time in your life, as you were then free from the wickedness of human tragedies and forced executions for your life to live.

You relieved yourself of that life and turned to God and the ministering of Immanuel's theistic philosophical beliefs in God, as you were asked to learn it for a better-gifted life with the integrity and wisdom bestowed upon you that you were sent to learn and practice in that life. It was a time when a man took an ancient universal faith to become a faith directly with God, then not known as Christianity, imposed by a faithful leader of God's will and well respected in his time as a minister, Immanuel, only many years later to be given the title "Jesus Christ."

" The name Jesus, the Greek meaning 'the delivered one,' and Christ, from the Greek word Christo, meaning 'the anointed one, ' and messiah of the established Christian faith. The new faith would adopt edicts of philosophies from Immanuel's ministering learnings derived from indirect Hebrew scriptures and Hindu and Buddhist ideological philosophies." I continued, hoping he understood. "Thus, came great and wonderful teaching, only later to be controlled by civilization's political interference and the established church hierarchy for indoctrination and domination as a slave church of the weak and non-believers to become only true believers in their ideology, the same as that of many other religions." I smiled and said," You and the family accepted a new balance of your lives from the inner gift of your souls by having the vision to express a heartened sensitivity and openness to others.

All was planned for a purpose for you to learn many things of mortal human life at its worst and then to accept a new way of life's peacefulness of love and sharing." "You shall not be judged as you have been told to believe; you shall enter eternal life's healing period to cleanse your spiritual soul and heart of all imposed unforgiving lectures and uncultured orders of you as a mortal human life." I smiled and said straight to him as he smiled and looked into my eyes. "Be at peace with yourself, be loving to all, and welcome home to your eternal life with all of us." Septimus' tears rolled down his face, and he smiled happily as I spoke. I assured him he would become so peacefully relaxed, gracious, and loving to all in the coming healing period, and learn many things about heaven and mortal life. You will learn through your healing that God did not nor would not send you on a mortal human journey for you to endure difficult experiences and then bring you home to discard you because of your experiences, but only express the learning of these experiences."

Shortly, you may again be asked to return to a new mortal life as a distinctive character for whatever reason God and the archangel may need him. For this was not the last of human lives to be lived. I stood and said. "All is well; you are now home, safe, and with God. I shall leave now and leave you with your guardian angels to prepare you for the periods of healing. Then, I shall meet you again in the future, and we shall share a wonderful, loving friendship as brothers and angels to help others."

Part III

One day, as usual, I was sitting on my veranda doing what I loved best in heaven, reading worldly scriptures and reviewing words and messages from earthly humankind civilization being imposed, increasing indoctrination upon citizens of different faithful beliefs, and the authorities assuring all is conducted.

Shaking my head in disbelief that such laws and rules of disgust could even be considered by a species of civilization that thought themselves to be intelligent and advanced, with the simplest of mathematics and limited science, further astounded me. But then I read of extraordinary peaceful individuals who work hard to bring an agreeable belief to others that are of God's will and teaching to accept one God as he, and understand the truth of the real creation and to assure nature edicts to survive and believe in the inner soul of their mortal life in a spiritual soul. This is when I know humanity is doing well without the insurgents of ideological indoctrination and dominance to satisfy egoism.

Once again, my peaceful contemplation was interrupted by the serving angel, bearing news of an angel seeking an audience with me. Curiosity piqued, I inquired about the visitor's identity. The serving angel's response only deepened the mystery: "He said you would recognize him when you see him, and he is most persistent to see you." With a mixture of anticipation and wariness, I granted the visitor entry, rising from my chair to greet him.

I had yet to learn who he was. I looked up, and it was still a colossal man of an angel, and immediately, I knew who it was. It was Septimus the gladiator, now an angel. I smiled with a full face and hugged my friend, as he was so delighted to see me as well. I stood and looked at him in pride and said how well he looked and, of course, younger as we all are once returning to eternal life. I said. "I guess I can no longer call you Septimus the Gladiator anymore." He laughed and said. "Yes, only you may call me that, for you knew my past life and assisted me during a challenging time, and for that, I am most grateful to you," I said. "And what shall we all call you now?" he smiled and said. "Well, I have as yet decided on a Heavenly spiritual name, nor has anyone come forth with any great suggestions. Therefore, I am willing to be received as I am, Septimus; the name was graciously given to me in my last mortal life; it seems to fit somehow." I smiled and laughed for a moment, and said. "You can be assured the name does have the means to provide you well in statute and grace. Welcome to my home, and make yourself comfortable." I requested the serving angel to bring refreshments. We sat, and I asked. So, how did your stay in the Healing Temple go, and what did you think?"

He sat for a minute, stared into the heavenly cosmos, then turned and said. "I was amazed at the healing process we as spiritual souls, once mortals, must go through to heal us and rid our spiritual souls of the mortal inconsistencies and wrongs to life itself so inflected by humanity and civilization, not to mention destructive atmospheres engulfing life with diseases.

This does not include the stress from a mental point of view, but also that of a physical statute, cleansing ourselves. I was stunned, now feeling reborn into a wonderful spiritual soul angel as one of God's children again and feeling so peaceful and happy with others I knew in my mortal life, and enjoying our friendships and love for each other." I smiled as he expressed his feelings for his new spiritual life as an angel. I could see and feel the energy of his happiness.

I held his hand and said how happy I was for him, especially for him to think of me and visit me with such excellent news. Now, he should understand that the mortal life experienced was not for a mortal human to seek a spiritual life and experience, as it was a spiritual soul seeking the experience of a mortal human's life, which God manifests for a reason.

He immediately bowed his head and lost his smile. He then looked up at me and said, "I did come with the significant healing information and wanted to share this happiness with you, but I have other news I am not yet so pleased about and need your guidance." I looked puzzled for a moment about what he could be talking about.

Finally, he looked me in the eyes and said, "I have to return to a mortal life again, and I have been told it may be in the future to the period in which I lived when you visited me. It seems there may be other lessons to life I must learn and deal with in the manner that mortals do while journeying, and even assist in guiding others. The archangels have said I will be living in the future in the ninth century.

I do not know what that means, what is planned for me and to whom I shall be born, or anything about their lives in this period." I looked at him in amazement and wondered why, so soon after returning from such a very harsh mortal life as a gladiator, he had to return in a period still seemingly uncivilized and not as advanced as the period he came six hundred years before.

Many questions need answers and guidance. I said, "Let me ask the archangel for more direction and what is planned for this new mortal journey and life you are expected to be born into." Septimus shook his head in agreement. He knew I could only obtain limited answers, even with my authority.

A few days later, I was finishing a meeting and gathering with the archangels. I asked Archangel Ariel to sit with me, and he could advise me of any information regarding Septimus's requirement to be sent on a new mortal life journey so soon after returning from the past one as a gladiator. Archangel Ariel smiled and said other lessons needed to be learned in life for better stability in characterizing being an angel, as he would be appointed one day.

I knew that was a heavenly circumvented answer, and he wouldn't be too forthcoming in providing accurate details of this particular life. Ariel looked at me and said, "Actually, you may know more than we do about the character; he shall be living on the Earth in the ninth century."

I looked at him in puzzlement and said. "I do not understand?" He turned and said. "He shall live in the same period you were asked to visit in the ninth century on your multi-journey in the past." I stopped for a minute, looked at him, and said. "May I ask the character's name when he shall be born and of what faith?' Ariel smiled and said. "I think you already know; you met him during your visit." I smiled and said. "If he is to be Jewish, then I accept your explanation unconditionally."

Ariel smiled and winked. He stood and turned and said. "You must realize that as the angel he shall become, he shall journey through several mortal lives in the time that is manifested for purpose, for he shall become a great teacher of human life from the past, and this alone prepares our newly spiritual souls for their coming human mortal lives." And he walked away. I smiled with happiness, for Septimus would be living a much better life in the ninth century than he had in the third century as a gladiator. However, it too would have its difficulties of multiple religious conflicts bringing harshness and death to others. But, when the new journey ended, he would return to eternal life as a completely different character, never to be called Septimus again, but rather by the new journey's character name to be given to him.

Once, I was home and relaxing after a full day of council with the high angels, as the high angels planned future peaceful living in the heavenly dimension. I motioned for my angel server to come over to where I was sitting. I said to him, "First, I wish for a refreshment; then I need you to contact the angel Septimus, who was here visiting me the other day, and request that he come to visit me as soon as possible."

The angel server nodded in acceptance and left. Later in the evening, Septimus arrived and was escorted out to the veranda, where I had just finished my dinner and was sipping a refreshment. I asked Septimus to please be seated. As he sat down and became comfortable, I said to him.

"I have spoken to the archangels regarding the up-and-coming mortal journey you will be living in the future." As I spoke, he looked very curious in a dead, still facial expression as to what I would reveal.

I continued. "I think you may be rather pleased with the little information I am allowed to know and further explain and unknowingly share with you what this is all about." That captured his attention. I smiled and said. "It is not as brutal a mortal life as you may think. It is in the ninth century, and you shall live in Jerusalem as a tavern keeper of the Jewish religion under Islamic occupation."

I expressed further. "If I were you, I think you should attend the heavenly library, study Judaism, and learn some of the languages, as well as some Arabic and some Latin. Only to become familiar with the cultural customs of several peoples, for there are going to be other journeys as well." He looked at me, stunned, and said. "That's all you can tell me?" I said. "That's all I know." I could not express to him what actually had taken place on my visiting journey during that period.

I reassured him, "Not to worry, it will not be as difficult a life as you once had in a past life." I paused for a moment and reminded him, "By the way, you shall not remember anything from your past life to carry forward into the new life, although you may catch yourself thinking you have experienced this before, it seems. Remember, the journeys are for your future goodness, to our eternal teachings, and what you can contribute to humanity." He smiled, stood up, and said. "Thank you. You have a way of making me feel more comfortable with this new adventure journey coming toward me. I appreciate the support and guidance you provide." I must leave, for I have so much to prepare for, and I assure myself I understand the manifested lessons I will learn from what experiences come my way in mortal life."

I smiled and blessed Septimus with God's will. Again, in the future, I shall see Septimus as several other mortal characters on a manifested journey that will have taken seeking lessons through experiences of understanding a new human life hosting his spiritual soul, only to transcend home to heal once again and to teach others preparing for their journeys. What he shall not understand while living the human mortal journey is that he will not remember or know of any past journeys he has ventured.

"May all mortal journeys be blessed."

THE THIRD STORY

Returning Home,

My Son Spiritual Soul of Islam

ابنى الإسلام

Praise be to God, For there is only one God, Allah.

My Son of Islam

ابنى الإسلام

I am watching the swirling shifting sands in the breezes flowing across the great desert hills of dunes.

The sands were covering the artistic hoof prints of faithful riding warriors from far away, all with signals of faithful flags imprinted with words of this new faith.

My son of Islam journeys across great lands of emptiness, conquering and seeking their people to teach the guiding words of God...and all his wisdom.

The tribes of the desert sands and their emptiness...live the knowledge of nature's creeds of life it gives...as they praise God's gift of life....Inshalla.

"If God wills it."

In its beginning, Gabriel, the Archangel, came to my son of Islam in dreams and spoke of new truths to live and bring a new faith. The one God of faith to all...in his lands.

For the words and teachings of Abraham were true to Allah.

With obedience to the sword as early barbarism, a faithful prophet teaches the faithfulness of six grand pillars to a peaceful life...as one in his soul seeks its wisdom and spiritual awakening.

"Allah Kareem"

Part I

In the Desert with a Nomadic Bedouin

I n the year 570 AD. Medina was a small village nestled in the Ibraham wadi bed valleys of the Sirat mountains in western Arabia. This was one of the first established village town settlements using tribal nomadic caravans, with a citizen population of approximately two thousand inhabitants, made up mostly of herders, agricultural farmers, and small store merchants selling their goods. All trading was conducted in the sandy dirt streets amongst the clay and limestone walls of their businesses and dwellings. The aroma was stagnant with animals' flesh hanging quarters for sale, and stands of fruits and vegetables could be seen to pick from as sheep and goats wandered around underneath the food stands while cooking means were already prepared for the hungry buyer. Even the mountains, not as high as others, provided a higher altitude of cool air in the winter months, but not in the heat of summer days. The area was ruled at the time by the Quraysh tribe of Yemeni further south in the city of Sana'a. A man was born into the world with a purpose, a mandated journey, Muhammad, to a father named Abdulla and a mother called Amina of the Kinana tribe. Both parents died when he was very young, and he was an orphan to be raised by his uncle. Muhammed did not attend any schools or lectures and was illiterate for life, unable to read or write. Any religion of the time was a mixture of Hebrew prophecies and Paganism of multi-God figures worshiped and preached in Arabic, Hebrew, some Greek, and a southern tribal dialect of Aramaic. Muhammed married a wealthy woman of the time and became a successful merchant in the city.

One day, Muhammed felt the need by the intervention of spiritual thoughts of alerted messages to walk and go up into the mountains where it is said he heard the first of revelations of God by the Arch Angel Jibrail (Gabriel) teaching words from ancient written scriptures, he listened to those of Abraham, Moses, Noah, and man called Jesus the true prophets and sons of God. It is noted that upon this journey of revelation, God revealed divine prophecies and teachings of Judeo-Christian traditions and ideological rituals, some eastern philosophies, Hinduism, and Buddhism, that had been most ministered by Immanuel, now titled Jesus Christ, during his ministry. Later, Muhammad would tell of such teachings as sacred in truth in the Qur'an of previous prophets, but felt he could not grasp the reality of the Old Testament and lost revelations in the five books of the Hebrew Torah/Tawrat. Although Muhammad, as written in the Qur'an long after his death, is said to be the son of God, the only true prophet of God is the only pathway to the Kingdom of Heaven. Muhammad had never come to understand and accept that he was only one of many sons of God and was not the only pathway to the truths of only one God.

Part II

A loud snorting sniffs awakened me, and the heavier snorts of an animal looking over me as I jumped to move away from this large camel stared back at me in absolute wonder as I, too, was wondering what and where it came from. It was early morning. I stood up and saw a herd of camels, goats, and a few sheep wandering around the pond, drinking and making terrible noises with the pleasure of drinking, quenching a needed thirst.

Then, I saw the figures of several people approaching me with curiosity as to what I was doing here in the middle of nowhere alone, as dangerous as the desert can be at times. I shook the sand and dust off me and waved as an older man approached me with a long staff, dressed in a long robe and headcover to protect himself from the upcoming morning sun and rising heat. The elderly man walked up to me and stared as he looked me up and down, and said," Madhaba, As-Salamu-Alaikhum." Immediately, I switched my speaking language to a simpler Bedouin dialect of Arabic. We approached each other and shook hands. He said to me. 'I am Braham-Iban-Muhammed, and this is my family; we are herders of the camels we buy and sell at the great camel caravan traders across this great desert." I smiled and bowed my head, and said. "I am Elijah Malachi, a messenger of the word of God." He looked at me at first with a strange look and said. "You must be an intellectual messenger of God." Braham was a man of Islam who had converted because he met the Prophet Muhammad in Medina on one of his many trips and learned of God, the one Allah of all humanity. I nodded with a smile and said.

"Praise be to Allah." He smiled and shook his head with acceptance. We sat after morning prayers and talked again of their travels to the waters known as the Gulf of Arabia in the eastern edges of the southern Arabian Peninsula, where other tribes and traders met with goods from faraway places across the land and seas, east and west.

Braham said there were people of black color who were the slaves of merchants and others from cultures from much further east of these lands, speaking in strange tongues with colorful dress and speaking of different faiths in the Gods they follow, unlike that of us here in our desert. He said he liked to trade for spices and cloth to bring back to the desert tribes on this side of the waters for people like himself and those of Islam. He said he came into tribes of Christians and Jews alike who have spoken of their religious faiths to a man named Jesus of a religion called Christianity, and, of course, the Jews who have been here for many years and spoke of Abraham. Braham looked at me and said. "In my travels to Medina and northern villages, I have been further into the northern great desert country and met many Jewish people who have descended from old Jewish families, and some had been slaves, now living in a mountainous area called Badr, Jebel al-Lawz. They say this is where Musa came with the Jews escaping from Egypt across the Sinai and shallow waters of the Gulf of Eilat many years before, and where Musa wrote and ministered to the twelve Jewish tribes his clay tablets of God's laws at the Mybayach. We walked on the hardened sand, stepping over and around rocks and admiring the cliffs' different layers of centuries of geological earth sediment colors as they stretched into the sky.

Braham said. "It's wonderful what Allah has created for us as a man on this earth; it's beauty and bountiful means for us to live." His statement at first took me, and then I knew he did give notes and blessings to God's creed and edicts of life. I replied. "Yes, God does wish for us as men first to understand as the creator all of the creations and all that nurtures us on this earth. And in the future of man as we learn more, gain the knowledge, and use the wisdom of God to see newer things of his creation for a better life for all." Braham smiled and said. " Elijah, you understand a great deal about Allah and what he does for man and ask interesting questions about my travels to learn more as I do each day." I smiled and replied. "I am learning about you, Braham, that you are a true spiritual soul seeking a mortal human experience in this life and its harshness it brings each day."

He smiled and shook his head, replying. "Yes, how true". The night grew dark and late as the others had parted to their tents to sleep for the night. I stood and reached out my hand to Braham and said Shukran, for your honest hospitality, "Allah Kareem: (may God always answer your prayers)." he pulled me over for a manly embrace and thanks. We both left each other's company and returned to our section of the main tent to sleep. I lay quietly until all were asleep. I left the tent, walked down to the water's edge next to a palm tree, sat down against it, and said my prayer. "Father, whom art in heaven, lay me down to sleep and bring me home, for I have completed this journey in your name." "L Alan Al-mein Amen." I fell asleep covered in my robe and blanket from the chilly desert night air.

Part III

The Vagabond's Return Home

I was strolling through one of the heavenly gardens, enjoying the beauty nature has brought us to witness and absorb into our lives. I was seriously eyeing the roses and other flowers closely as I could feel their beauty and the truthfulness of their vibrant colors of life to us. Nature has many things to offer everyone's life in all living dimensions, from its evolving beauty to its fruits of nurture supporting other life, as all are related.

The trees shaded me from the bright sun as I read scriptures and daily words of wisdom from our teachers. I saw an older man with a long white beard dressed in a robe and headdress sitting in meditation on a bench, his head bowed, thumbing a string of worry beads.

As I approached and looked closer, I could see that it was Braham, the Bedouin camel herder and trader I had met on my journey to the sixth century in the Arabian desert. I stopped and said. "Braham." he looked up at me with a surprised look to see Elijah, the messenger from God. He stood, bowed, and cupped his hands around mine to thank God for our chance meeting. He said. "Oh! Thank Allah, you are here. I had wondered so many times in life where you went when you left my encampment of herders. As you see, I am here now in Heaven. I passed over a few days earlier, and angels came and assisted me in transcending here with many others the same day. I am an old man now and weak. I do not know what I am supposed to do here." I smiled back and said.

"I know you must feel lost right now, but have no fear. You are in heaven with God, your prophet Mohammed of Islam, and many others like you, who guided you in your mortal life. You shall attend all the healing of mortal life in the Healing Temple as everyone does upon transcending from mortal life." He felt more relaxed and comfortable having me there to comfort his thoughts. I said to him. "Please sit and let me hear of your travels and life after I visited you some time ago in the desert, where you treated me with profound respect and honor as your guest." As we sat on the bench, he smiled with a gleam and twinkle in his eyes and said.

" Oh, we all were surprised when we awoke, and you were gone from us that morning. We all missed you. We caravanned north to Medina and then Mecca, a newer settlement for the Islamic Hajj, to meet my grandson, whom I told you was studying there." I shook my head, acknowledging him telling me about his son in a religious teaching school.

He suddenly looked, unfortunately, saddened in his face; it seemed to droop from the smiles of happiness. Braham looked up at me and said. "My grandson, Kaleel-Braham Iban Muhammed, was murdered before we arrived in Medina." He sobbed as tears streamed from his old eye with great sorrow. I looked at him in surprise, for I had not seen his grandson in the healing temple. I asked. "How did this happen?" He looked up at me and said. "He refused to join a radical Islam group of young boys and men to overthrow the school he attended for not teaching the true wisdom of Muhammad in a peaceful means of God and accused him of being possessed by a Hadith Jinn."

Further, the insurgents called in a Raqi to exorcise him unwarrantedly, who said he could not be cured, so they beheaded him in a public square." I said. "You know there is evil in many people with different beliefs in God, and these religions separate by any means those who do not believe as they do and those who chose to be evil and carry out evil things are in this mortal life for just that purpose: to learn a lesson from their wrongdoing toward humankind eventually. They shall be going through a prolonged period of healing. As long as your grandson carries in his heart the spirit of God, he shall be enlightened here in the eternal life." I asked. "Have you seen him or looked for him here yet?" He replied. "No, I do not know where to look or whom to ask," I said. "I know how and to whom to inquire, and we shall find him for you to reunite again." I held him in comfort, understanding his pain. He was not caring for himself or the transcending he had just come through, as he was concerned about his grandson. He turned to me and said. "Thank you. I am honored to have you here with me. I should have been in Medina and Mekka sooner to defend and help my grandson. Years ago, I pledged to God and Mohammed that I would protect my grandson with all my life for him to grow into a fine young man and not have to live as a nomadic boudin as his family has for hundreds of years." I said to him. "This is not your fault, as it is part of his life's plan, but it became more sudden than expected by those spiritual souls seeking mortal life who yet have found their meaning and true loving purpose to their mortal lives as you have.

You shall learn this more deeply while healing at the temple and become more spiritual in your spiritual life here in eternity. The religions you have experienced and witnessed are based on great fear and restriction; here in the eternal life, we as spiritual souls are founded on love for each other and divine freedom." I smiled and further said. "Behold your healing with boundless joy, for you shall meet with all spiritual leaders and teachers and receive God's blessings and be welcomed home. And yes, you shall meet many other friends you once knew in mortal life and see your grandson." I stood and offered my hand to him with a smile and said. "Come, I shall walk you back to the Healing Temple." Braham stood up with a smile and wiped his tears for his sorrow of losing his grandson, and we strolled down the path leading to the great Healing Temple. As we walked, I reminded Braham of what we had once talked about during my visit to the desert when he was born. He could express his loving sensitivity for his family and fellow man and how, as a Bedouin nomad, he brought stability while wandering the desert, honestly trading with many other cultures' faiths in God. This was all part of his mortal journey, and his opinion of meeting these character goals as one of God's children would be asked during the healing period. He smiled and said. 'I tried in God's name to be the best of everything I knew to share and pray all is well."

A few days later, I entered the Healing Temple as requested to visit other spiritual souls transcending to their eternal spiritual life. I was emotionally upset with the suddenness felt by many who had passed from mortal life and awakened in a new dimension.

I was always asked to aid with such cases, bring each into the new world of eternal spiritual life, and shed their emotions of life they will never have to experience again as the character they had lived. Other angels directed me to a few spiritual souls who had arrived. Within the temple, a sense of unity and love permeated the air. We, the spiritual souls, were all connected, bound by a common purpose.

We expressed our kindness and love for each other, our angelic brotherhood, as we prepared for our journey to heaven. Then, I wandered off into other areas of the temple, where teaching and healing meditations were taking place. The beautiful, loving teaching of the four veils by the seven sands, by the seven archangels of life, explained issues of mortal life they all had endured and why.

But more importantly, how to shed the spiritual soul of human guilt and deadly civil laws and restrictions through indoctrination into their conscience, and feel free in this new heavenly eternal life. Further, to share their hearts' love for each other without fear, many were so imbued with an untruthful ideology of true faith in God that they feared him but were ordered to love him.

Teaching a new spiritual soul with such inept indoctrination was challenging to love to instill that God was never to be feared, for he loved all his children. Yet, each would take their own time in healing to understand that placing fear of God was a mortal means of domination. I could see the facial expressions of some who were so excited about their new spiritual life, and they smiled and sang out grace and praises to God, and held onto and hugged each other. Seeing and feeling their free love and an angel was a wonderful, loving sight. In another room, I saw Barham sitting now dressed in an all-white robe and looking much younger than he did in the past, and was seated next to a young man, smiling and singing out with the greatness of joy as they, at times, would reach over and hug. I walked up and said. "Braham?" He turned and jumped up with a smile and said. "Oh, thank you, God! I have met my grandson and am so pleased as he motioned for his grandson to rise to come to meet me." He then shouted. "Kaleel, this is my friend, the angel Elijah, a messenger from God, who came and visited me many years ago in the desert and was teaching me about the four veils of God's word." Kaleel smiled, shook my hand, and said. "Thank you for bringing my grandfather here to me." I smiled with joy when they found each other and said. " Once I knew you were here, I enquired and knew you would meet again and reunite your grandfather and grandson's love for each other; now, you both have a wonderful, eternal life together." They both smiled and sat back down to listen to their teaching, for they shall be in the temple of healing a while longer before living out in heaven as other angels and with assignments as well, all have in keeping with our Heavenly Dimension, the wonderful loving place for eternity for all. Knowing it was now a wonderful reunion between Braham and his grandson, I could still see in his mind that he had no idea we had met before in one of his past lives. In early transcending and processing through the heavenly healing temple of spiritual soul healing, one's conscience and subconscious do not reflect any other mortal lives one may have lived. While journeying through human life, it is rare but possible to instantly gain subconscious thoughts in the moment of a possible reenactment of an experience. After completing his healing process and slowly entering the angels' world of eternity, Braham would later start to regain his memories of different mortal lives and understand these lives' purposes.

On my centuries-long journey through several periods, meeting people of other faiths and religions, Brahman was my third person, but in the sixth century, I met. "My Son of Islam" yes, Braham from the sixth century, the Bedouin nomad, named Braham, or now to be Shi in another journey, as one may choose to praise him, was in each life for learning and experiencing God's selected lessons and understanding God's four veils and principle spiritual laws. In one life, he accepted Islam from Mohammed, and now, in the eighth century, two hundred years later, he adopted the religion of Buddhism as a devout Buddhist student of a local Xuanzang priest believer in the Tika and Madhu-Tika writings, wandering the mountains of Tibet. God foresees the wisdom of many spiritual mortal journeys in all his children.

*Centuries from "Allah Kareem" to "Behold now,
Bhikkhus, I exhort you."*

THE FOURTH STORY

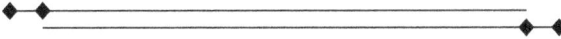

*Returning Home,
My Son Spiritual Soul of the Hebrew*

שלי הבן את העברית

Selicha

127

MY SON, THE HEBREW

שלי הבן את העברית

Wrapped in the holiest of sacred tallit's ... bowed at the wall of tears, reciting Kedushah to Yah...
As life's strengths from the monolithic wall of stone in faithful silence so conquered and lost from centuries past,
My faithful son of the Hebrew chants with praise, reciting prayers of Salvation and Daat from the tablets of life's laws...
A covenant union between myself, the divine, and he.
Ever so settled in a rhythm of life's contributing balances,
The spiritual faith of divine immanence of me...

"Thy will be done." ...

Forever away from an exodus in the travesty of dominion and not left wondering in lost paths of the deserts...
For the lost souls of many kindred tribes faded into other's evil dominion for the sacrifice of world orders....a life now passed and left in peace by Shamash.
Only to be read in the etched carvings of a grand tapestry to one's sacred history...forever sung in an oration by enigmatic teachings in celebrated tongues.
The teachings of actual knowledge of wisdom, edicts of nature, and enlightened awareness of your soul. For they shall never be feared as I am loved.

For I have moved this universe into a new orb of brilliant life of lights, seeing the truths of me.

Oh Hebrew, my son of strength, go forth with your gentle hand and staff to speak the truths of life's laws and renowned divinity of my salvations....to affirm Shema Yisrael.

Fear, not the spoken darkness of dominion from others or the encrypted mystic writings of falseness to you, my creations, are the chosen ones.

I am no mystery to humanity and the highest spirits with dominion over all things.

Come forth and speak to me your prayers and divine thoughts to protect thy only soul and answer life's quests....to be in perfect unity to living kindness.

Kindness to all your soul and minded body, self-awareness, and enrichment of the life I gave you to live shall give you eternity until it's time to rest.

For in time... life's eternal rest shall fall upon you ...and you shall return to me...in a recalling of life as the spiritual being You are...my faithful son, the Hebrew...

Kneeling in praise and thanksgiving for this life's outward boundaries brought into truths harmony to say...the daath of life's experiences shall be unjudged in the righteousness of your life's guided reasonings. It is a journey of true worth in itself.

Therefore, come...travel across my great lands to meet your brothers, celebrate our life's garden in the desert, and listen to my truths told to all.

My son...the Hebrew....

"Selicha"

My Son, Spiritual Soul, the Hebrew of Jerusalem

*L*ife in Jerusalem was like that in many other cities, with dirt and stone-paved streets, a pathway next to the buildings of dwellings, and small merchant shops selling wares and foods for the populous. Arabic and Hebrew were the main languages, as Islam was the enforced religion, with mosques being built. Islamic Sharia laws were applied to all, no matter your religious faith, with strict guidelines and controls in place. The Jews were still allowed to practice their faith in synagogues as in the previous year; at times, migrant Jews were forbidden even to enter the city, only those considered current residents. The Temple Mount, the Dome of the Rock, was no longer a Jewish holy shrine but was converted to an Islamic holy place for prayer. For a time, both religions accepted each other and allowed simple rituals of celebration. The region was under Islamic laws and rules, and at times, smaller settlements caused unrest due to the harsher treatment of local citizens. This in itself would ignite the Christian rebellions, which mostly were put down at once by Muslim Holy forces, as the words spread to the west into Europe and Rome, the lead city for the Roman Catholic churches ruled by the Pope of the time.

Part I

I walked up to the fountain, splashed water on my face, and drank from its clear waters, again thirsty from my long walk into the city. I sat on the fountain edge and looked around, seeing life as it is on this day and remembering it as it was almost a thousand years ago. The exception of change was that no Roman soldiers were marching through, only Muslim Mattawa's religious enforcers, assuring Muslims to pray.

I walked down several streets, not knowing exactly where I was going, just seeing more buildings built for the Islamic religion and even crossing the front steps of a Jewish synagogue. I found it almost unnoticeable from the outside. Still, as I entered through the doors, it was beautifully decorated inside, with an altar supporting the Shabbat with candles and dim oil lamps around an open-air room with carpets and chairs or benches to sit in. I sat on a bench in the quiet of the cool, peaceful room and thought about the start of my day until this moment, resting myself in a relaxed, meditative manner to gather myself. It wasn't long before a man dressed in robes and headdress approached me, looked at me momentarily, and asked in Hebrew. From here on, we would speak in the Jewish language of Hebrew. "Who are you, and why are you here? Are you Jewish?' I smiled and said. " Shalom, I am Elijah Malachi, a traveler and messenger of God. I came into one of God's houses of prayer to rest and give thanks for this day." He quickly stepped forward and said. "But you are a vagabond with dirty clothes and unkept smelling of goat, and you call yourself a messenger of God?" In his almost angry voice. He further said. "I am Rabbi Samuel, living here as the head of the synagogue for prayer. You must leave if you are not Jewish, for others are forbidden to enter here." Again, even in a more stern, angry voice of disgust. I looked at him and said. "I am tired and only resting my feet while I visit this place of God's prayer and sanctuary of peacefulness." I looked him in the eyes and said in a pleasant tone. "If I pray to God, will he listen to me here, and Abraham deliver my prayer to him even though I am not Jewish?" He looked back at me and said. "If you are a man of God, you know as I do that he will always listen to his children and more so to the chosen ones of Israel, for we are the truest way to heaven."

I smiled and said. "I heard these same words from the Imam of Islam and again from the followers of Jesus Christ in the Christian religion. But I ask, which of you is correct?" This angered him more, and he bitterly stared at me. He said nothing as he looked at me with wonder and said. "Of course, we Israelites are the only true faith, according to Abraham." I stood up and stretched for a minute, and said. 'Shlom geta bout, thank you for your kindness; I shall depart now that I am rested." He followed me to the doors and shut them strongly behind me as I walked out. As I walked away, mentally, I knew this character was ignoring his true mandated journey of being a Rabbi, continuing as a mortal human seeking a spiritual experience rather than having his spiritual soul seek the truly human life's experience he was sent to live. Instead, he hid behind a false impression of spirituality. Seeking my own continued journey, I walked down the old streets of Jerusalem just as if I knew where

I was going, not having any idea of direction except for the driven thought to walk and explore. I walked much further, and in astonishment, there was this grand opening into a magnificent plaza with a great building in the center with a golden dome. The building was a beautiful, large stone and marble structure, the largest I had ever seen in this part of the world. As I walked closer, I could see Guards all around it and a sign in Arabic scripted graphics, the Dome of the Rock, a place of Islamic prayer considered holy because it was said Muhammad had come there to pray and be blessed in the name of Allah. The Dome Rock was a wonderful place for Islam, but even more so for the Jewish and Christian religions. There was a mosque called Al-Aqsa, also beautiful in design, with open air for prayer, covered in Bedouin-weaved carpets from Arabia and the lands of Persia. Traditionally, I stepped up to the water near the mosque doors and washed my feet and face before entering the grand building.

I was amazed at the beauty and painted words on the upper walls in Arabic, saying words of Islam and praise unto one God, and that of only one God. I walked in on the beautiful felt carpets on my feet and stared at everything.

As I walked closer to view the walls, a man dressed in robes and a fancy headdress approached me and said, "Who are you? It was not time for prayer this afternoon; the call to prayer shall come later." He held out his hand and said, "Salom Alaikhum." I crossed my heart with this traditional Islamic welcoming gesture.

I returned the welcoming gesture as well with a smile. Here is an Islamic religious place, and I had to speak Arabic to him. He asked who I was. I said. 'I am Elijah, visiting Jerusalem and came to admire the mosque and the wonderful Dome of the

Rock." He looked at me and said, But you are a vagabond with no means of importance and a beggar and asked if I were Muslim. I bowed my head and said. "No, I am not Muslim; I am a man of God's faith and a messenger." He looked stunned and backed away momentarily, and said I was not a holy man of Islam or any religion, and I am then an infidel and must leave this sacred ground is only for the true believers in Muhammad and God only. I turned and started walking out, for I knew I was not only allowed in the mosque but did not want to be the lowest of men in his eyes of Islam. I departed the Mosque and stepped back into the fresh air of the season. After such walks through the city, I started feeling hungry. I walked further and saw a coffee tavern on one corner and decided to walk in and ask if I could clean the floors for a loaf of bread or even half a loaf in return for food, enough to fill my hunger needs. I could see from markings on the outer walls that this is a Jew-owned shop. I walked in and asked for the proprietor, who looked at me from a distance and curiously walked over to enquire about my request.

I said. "Shalom," and asked if I could clean his floors for food. He looked at me for a minute, shook his head with a smile, and said. "Yes, my brother, and please clean the tabletops as well." He directed me to the back to collect a broomstick with straw wrapped in cloth, rope at one end, and a rag to clean the tables. I laid my staff up against the wall, walked back into the main room, and began sweeping the half-dirt and tile-covered floor. As I moved to clean, he asked my name. I turned and said. "My name is Elijah Malachi." And he said. "Where is it are you from?' I answered. "I am a traveler visiting this great land and city to learn its ways," I said. "What master is your name?" he smiled and said. " My name is Abraham, the son of Lucas from here in Jerusalem, a family of many centuries. I have owned this

135

coffee tavern all my life and inherited it from my father and his father and his father through all the years." I smiled and said. "You are blessed to have a wonderful establishment." He said. "Yes, my wife, now passed, may God rest her soul, helped me by baking the bread as I make and serving the coffee and tea from many faraway lands." I kept sweeping and cleaning the tabletops as I passed each one. Soon, I was finished, and Abraham brought me a mug of coffee with goat's milk, half a loaf of wheat bread fresh from the oven, and a slice of goat cheese and churned goat butter to share. I felt like I was back in heaven with a feast before me. I said. "Thank you, and I asked God to bless my food and Abraham for sharing this food with me." Abraham smiled and walked away. As I sat there eating and enjoying my food, I heard several people running up the street, screaming that the city was going to be invaded by an army outside the city's walls surrounding the whole city.

Part II

There was great confusion in the streets as we could see the Islamic Army and Jewish guards running toward the city's walls. Abraham and I stood at the doorway and watched, and he asked a passerby. "What is happening, and what is with all the screaming?" The man looked with a scared, startled face and said there was a great army surrounding the city, and they were a Christian Crusading army with flags of Christian, red-painted crosses. They are killing the citizens, Jews, and Arabs outside the walls and burning their dwellings." Abraham and I looked at each other, startled, returned to the tavern, and closed the doors. Abraham seemed very worried and said. "The Muslims have controlled Jerusalem for hundreds of years and scarcely allowed us Jews to practice our faith while not allowing the Christians to exist or have places of worship. Now, a large Christian Crusading army surrounds the city to invade us. The Christians despised the Muslims and Jews and would destroy this city or all of its citizens, only to control the region with Christianity."

Part III

Having managed to escape the city and now safe in the countryside at Abraham's brother's farm, we could see the fire and smoke of Jerusalem in the distance. It was a time when we knew from history that Nehemiah would have to return to rebuild Jerusalem, as he had five hundred years before. Abraham, Absalom, and I stayed still, chatting about his faith, the goodness of it all for humanity, and the true proclamations of God's words. I knew that after our talks, they were incredible men to teach the new generations the absolute truth of God, and their life's journey would be fulfilled with great rewards of kindness and blessings from God, for they truly understood faithfulness, even in a hard-felt time as this history of humanity. They both excused themselves as they left to sleep for the night. I remained up for a few minutes as I decided to walk outside and enjoy more fresh night air.

As I stood outside viewing the night sky, in the distance, the city of Jerusalem burned, and large plumes of smoke rose above. I could also see the heavenly angels lifting the spiritual souls of each mortal human that had been killed and transcending with them into heaven, for the mortal journey had unexpectedly ended abruptly in a brutal way. At that moment, one angel stopped, turned, and stared at me as she moved closer to me in wonder. The angel saw me as a senior angel in mortal life and knew I was there for a purpose; the angel bowed its head in honor of me with a smile and a sign of blessings and moved away to complete its task of gathering spiritual souls to transcend back to eternal life.

I walked over to the stables where the animals were in for the night, some sleeping and others still eating and wondering why I should come into their domain and stir them at night. Finally, I found a quiet place to lie in the hay, lie down to rest, and relax meditatively as I said my prayers and asked God to return me home for my visit here with our son was done. The Hebrew journey was complete. He knew the truthfulness of faith and guidance he would teach through the generations while in his life's journey. I fell asleep without issue and felt so at peace.

Part IV

The Vagabond's Return Home

Walking through the sacred forest, taking in the aroma of the flowers, and listening to the breeze singing through the trees, just enjoying the morning as we would every morning in heaven, I looked forward to seeing many new spiritual souls returning home from their journeys as mortals. Finally, I reached the outer smaller gardens of the Healing Temple when a servant angel approached me and asked if I had known a Jewish mortal named Abraham on one of my journeys. I looked up, quite surprised, and said. "I knew a wonderful Jewish tavern owner on my last journey to Jerusalem."

The angel looked at me and said, "He has returned from his mortal journey and now is the spiritual soul of eternal life, and he is asking for you." I motioned him on and said. "I shall be there shortly." The angel turned and left, returning to the temple.

I entered the temple, stopping to answer questions and give directions to the receiving and serving angels, who were accepting newly arriving spiritual souls returning from their mortal journey. Some felt unrestful in their transcendence, and others smiled in relief from the life they came from, while others looked wondrously at where they were.

On certain days, we knew in heaven when life was more difficult than on other days by the number of returning spiritual souls that came home. The worst days were when mortal beings engaged in wars and inflicted hideous deaths upon innocent people.

I remember Abraham saying that we were fleeing that day during the siege. "The religious atrocities of civilizations consume the faithful perils of humanity like the beasts in nature that nourish us."

Those days were the most difficult for all of us. I made my way into another room, quieter and more peaceful, where I saw an older spiritual soul sitting quietly, focusing on the bright light. God was sending his love and warmth to those coming home. As I approached, Abraham turned, looked up at me, stood, embraced me with tears of happiness, and said. "Thank God! Now I know I am home." I smiled and said. "Welcome home, my friend; for now, you are with God and all of us in the most peaceful place for eternity.

How do you feel?" Abraham looked at me with a bit of wonder and asked. "So, when shall I be judged for my mortal life, and when shall I learn of my fate to remain in heaven or be expelled?"

I smiled and said. "You have lived an extraordinary life as a Jewish man in Jerusalem during a terrible occupation of the radical Islamic world and ending with the dominance of the warring Christian rulers, but here you can practice your faith toward God quietly, our faith, not that of any religion. You even continued teaching your faith and the integrity and wisdom of the four veils of God's words as I delivered the message on my visit." I continued. "You shall not be judged for your life nor think you would go to any other place that does not exist, but only in mystic mindlessness. You shall enter the temple of healing as all do to cleanse the spiritual soul of mortal indoctrinated impurities, yourself of all wrongs and misdoing of mortal life imposed as judgments for their dominance by human civilization, and you have re-entered the glorious life of heaven for eternity with all of us. You were a true spiritual soul seeking a mortal human life experience as manifested, and you did well." Abraham smiled with a beautiful gleam in his eyes, and I could see the relief and relaxing moment as he sat back down. I said. "One day in the future, we shall meet again when you have become the angel you are, and we shall chat about everything you have experienced in mortal life. While attending the lectures in the healing temple, you were born into the life you experienced for a reason, one of faith, teaching, and channeling God's wisdom and knowledgeable trust to others with vision.

Then Abraham turned, smiled, and said. "I did try to teach and express God's love to all who would listen with acceptance," I said further to him. "You also were given the most prestigious honor of being direct and expressing honesty to all you taught God's word and the four main veils. So, while healing from the unpleasantness in mortal life inflicted upon your mortal being, remember that all you have is faith, which shall carry you into the eternal joys of heavenly life." I turned and mentioned. "I shall be looking for you soon, blessed be." Abraham spent less time in the healing temple than many others for his excellent heart as a mortal being, and later became a receiving angel to help others transcend home to heaven. We met many times after discussing life as we enjoyed it in heaven and the lessons once as mortal beings while on our journeys.

All along, he never remembered this was a second journey he had experienced, for he did not reflect on a past life as a Gladiator in Rome during the third century, as I had visited him then as well.

The memories of all the characters in different mortal lives are only sometimes remembered for a cause, as some may be remembered. These past lives are never remembered while on a human journey from the past, for it may disrupt the manifested cause of the current journey. In saying this, there can be moments of instant thoughts of a character in similar experiences that give such thoughts of possibilities of past lives. Again, one shall journey into the many millennia of humanity. The spiritual soul's manifested journey into the mortal human life experience is a need for all eternal spirits of heaven to teach the understanding of a continuously evolving human species.

The evolution of this human species evolves generation by generation in the more modern period than that of two thousand years earlier, and certain in the prehistoric moments of early human mortal life. Each of us, as angelic spiritual souls, should thank the Surrogate mortal human characters; we lived for each has given us knowledge and great wisdom of future lives to be lived in peace.

The Theories of "End of Times"

*T*hroughout humanity, the wonders of establishing the universe and the planet Earth remained a phenomenon, causing myths of many civilizations to contemplate which of the many Gods made the "ALL." As asserted in the beginning, the universe was not without symmetry of organizational hierarchy of elements that occur by cause and circumstantial consideration, with conditions of infusion or by immersion of physical force with opposing poles. In a sequence of analogous positive and negative frequencies, possible gravitational forces formed planets as they did by a suggestive cause of elements fast-moving through the universe. All newly forming planets are afire from celestial molten rocks cooling in the outermost cosmic atmospheres into a geologically formed sphere by centrifugal energy and gravitational force as a land mass to be its hardened surface, only later to be divided into continents. Possible agglomeration events occurred as planets gave credence to the universal gravital orbital placement around the center, Sun, and obliquity rotation about each other. Planet Earth is one that settled in its evolutionary epic period with atmospheric conditions suitable for living organisms. Only then could there be an existence? As humanity evolved after many other living creatures had existed, some then no longer exist; with the conscious curiosity of the "ALL" and witnessing the birth, life, and ending of other created creatures, nature's law of compliance became evident to death.

Humanity constantly wonders about their ending and that of Earth, only to become known as "The End of Times," created by mythical scenarios of eschatologies.

As religion emerged, philosophical ideologies became prevalent to humankind as civilizations demanded dominance, such fantastical eschatological scenarios enacted a much more important influence on man's concepts of varying myths. Throughout the millenniums of humanity, written scriptures in all beliefs of eschatology, the end of times is considered a trepidation of interest. But how? This shall remain an unanswered phenomenon throughout time until the future if it occurs. With the evolution of time and the achieved knowledge, humanity has evolved with improved logical ideological concepts that are more conclusive than the mythical theological ideologies portrayed in unsure scriptures and indoctrinated mindsets. Therefore, what is the end of times? Does the future of humanity mean God, our creator, no longer chooses to have a creative human creature evolve, or will there no longer be a universe or an Earth? From a logical theoretical point of simplicity, the subsequent interpretation possibilities can be considered for End of Times, for many more are still unknown. What is the End of Times? One must consider the possibility of the end of times as an evolutional concern since, as science has proven in history and to modern times, the earth's evolutional extinction is an ongoing process. Humanity knows to date history of earth's living creatures, and humanity has been through as many as six different forms of extinction epics.

The individual End of Times: The end of time can be related to each mortal human life's journey. For all human life shall end, meaning impermanent as manifested. Journeys are only a period in which the spiritual soul resides within its host, a mortal human, acting as the surrogate conduit for the spiritual soul, living its life experiences. The end of this mortal life assures the return of the spiritual soul as it shall be eternal, where the mortal human organic physical body returns to the earth for the final purpose of nurturing. As we know, the spiritual soul shall live through several such lives and individual end of "that" time. The end of "that' time other than a naturally induced death by uncivilized inhuman acts or by human biological and environmental causes. Never let it be misunderstood the current species of homo sapiens in their existing character form could not become extinct to a higher form of humanity; the possibility could exist.

The Human Intervention within Civilizations End of Times: Through evolved knowledge with an intellect without wisdom, humanity, by its act of cause, shall give credence to the destruction of itself, with repercussions to the natural environment. Such a reaction, causing a destructive annihilation, shall impose the self-inflicted end of times for civilization and possibly all living things.

The Earth's Self-imposed End of Times: We know through our limited and ever-evolving knowledge of the universe and accompanying planets how Earth was formed from celestial-infused causes of molten celestial debris. As the outer surface was cooling from the universal atmosphere, centrifugal force caused layered sedimentation formations in the generality of unconformity. At the same time, the inner core remains a collective celestial debris and its gaseous natural inferno. The earth's surface, a land mass, is divided by tectonic plates with its volcanic release of the inner core's inferno of molting debris and subsequent gases pressurizing releases. These actions release subterranean pressures, can provide newly created surface land mass, and or destroy civilizations as an opposite effect. The action could move forward in two directions for an end-of-time scenario. Earth's surface destruction could be possible if the inferno were to become greater than expected and cause an inner planet explosion, destroying all life and total extinction. As an opposite action and reaction, the inferno may extinguish itself by imploding, eliminating all causes of inner warmth.

This would leave the surface reliant upon a solar energy source to dominate in the interim as a terminating global glaciation event that ends at all times. In the current millennium, the depletion of historic fossil elements could become a rapid means of civilizations' decline and, within itself, cause an end-of-time extinction effect.

The Universal Cause of End of Times: The infinite cosmos is saturated with stars, asteroids, superflares, exploding supernovae, and other errant elemental debris moving through the universe's growth.

Even worse is an unexpected collapse, the Big Rip scenario of the Earth's magnetosphere creating dark energy, pulling elements further away, and voiding light energy as the universe expands. Human-evolved knowledge has developed methods to view as many of these elements as possible concerning Earth's solvency and protecting all of humanity and living things. Another possible cause for a cosmic element of substantial mass directing itself in force toward Earth and impacting the Earth is a significant possibility of life's annihilation, causing the end of time. History has proven such events and existing different possibilities of an apocalypse over the millennia. Extinction events occur during every millennial and century by different means than those of modern times. Currently, the Holocene extinction event is ongoing. Why? It seems even humanity, Earth's caretaker, is at fault as well in the evolutionary civilizations' intellectual growth of earthly elements and nature's proven plantations subsidies to live. Various earthen species have rapidly become extinct over the millennia. Therefore, evolutionarily, extinction occurs daily in all millennia.

The Celestial Immutable Spiritual Cause of End of Times: God, our creator, created the universe, the planets, especially Earth, and humanity with his spiritual conception from the many elements of the earth, as he did all other living creatures, as a sustainable life upon his earth. Knowingly, all living things are in their specific variation as a species of their time and millennial environment to evolve. As a human mortal created to be a surrogate for the spiritual souls' journey on several manifested life cycles through all of the millennia to begin human civilization and nurture the earth for sustainable life. Spirituality is conceivable for a reason or purpose, and has an "End of Times" if all spiritual journeys were suspended. If so, why even have a living planet named Terra with so many different species of life and only one to foster the growth of heavenly, immutable spiritual souls? Do other living creatures have souls?

God, the Almighty, will never destroy his living world. From human knowledge of their creation approximately three and a half million years ago, humans evolved into one specific homo-sapiens, an erectus species, directly from their evolving creation of species, so very different from Hominidae. The theological question remains from all faiths believing in the eschatological ideology of the "end of times." Why would God annihilate all living matter he created for a specific reason? In the theistic scriptural sense, composed as a mythical, immortally dramatized scripture, would God truly descend to his earth from the celestial heavens before such destruction is enacted? God needs his created world and all that's living upon it. God shall keep the planet and humanity in its current and continued evolved self for all living creatures. In reality, the complete annihilation, not impossible, but most unlikely, of earthly life would have to be from one or more of the other end-of-time theorized possibilities. Of course, theistic ideology has dramatized even this possible event by exerting an indoctrinated verse assuring God, preventing any end-of-time occurrence.

"For all of life is an orbital evolution for a reason."

Epilogue

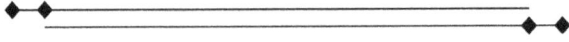

"For I have wept upon the sands in my path, I leave behind me."

I n the unembodied, immutable celestial, spiritual presence throughout the infinite universe, our creator unambiguously formed a world in his newest created orbital cosmos, a subsisting sphere, proclaimed as Terra (Earth). Why? It is planned to be an atmospheric environment for "ALL" living things that move and remain tranquil with growth to sustain their being. Manifested with a cause in support of everything "ALL" that surrounds in every way. Sustainable life from nativity through its evolution of vivacity until wilt ends its life span, its journey, only to decay into terrains supporting soils nurturing all others, declaring the cycle "dust to dust." One component of Earth was missing: an overseer of the continuing evolutionary process of Earth's life and acting as a conduit for celestial, spiritual souls to journey. Therefore, God extracted from the created Earth many mutable biochemical elements to sculpture a form, a figure to be a living being, not in his unembodied immutable spiritual image, but rather that of the physical existence of Earth's organic elements, to become known as an anthropocentrism to nurture the created allotment of all living things. God did so by creating the first, not as the mythical theistic beliefs conceived, but rather that each to be an evolutionary Anthropocene custodian, surviving a precedent intervention to evolve through the many evolutionary cycles of Earth would experience. Beginning in southeast Alkebulan, the true evolutionary mystic garden of human origin. Therefore, several living beings appeared tangibly only in their evolutionary period, similar but unique for a cause manifested for a reason, unlike or from any other living Hominidae creature. God extended a celestial, spiritual gift to each human species as the first creature of its kind with a spiritual soul as part of himself, "The Holy Spirit," to perform, experience the moments of life, gain knowledge, cause, and evolve through Earth's future. All future spiritual souls gifted shall be spiritually allied with their character in humanity on earth as both evolve.

Plagiarizing a theistic, scripted mythical ideological narrative of the first living beings, supposably consuming nature's fruits, offered an imposing relational, emotional ethics operative consciousness in pleasantry or maliciousness to adopt upon each experience. Humanity was conscientiously able to determine a path of tranquility or that of injustice during its manifested mortal journey only through guilted judgment. The insight of a knowing or unawareness of the conciseness of experiencing life is an awakening to the betterment of humanity

151

as a living community. God only asked in his greatest wisdom and thoughtfulness for all of humanity to exist in his loving harmony of belief and honor in him and appreciation of all nature's provisions to sustain their lives, as of all created.

As importantly, believing in the enlightenment in themselves and knowing the inner spiritual soul of God that lives within themselves gave the human body a functional life and consciously guided them. Within the thoughts of wisdom came the four veils, where the seven sands of life's creativity taught knowledge of a rationalized existence of humanism. The evolution of humanity applying the conscious mind accepted the Four Veils and Seven Sands as a pleasing means of life, while many others manipulated precedence as a sinister hegemonic manner of false pleasantry or imposed maliciousness befitting an ever-growing populous civilization. God sent many of his sons to give comfort in the true faith of the Four Veils with philosophical verses and psalms of wisdom in peace for a day's life. When each humanoid has ended their mortal journey, the spiritual soul shall transcend to the cosmos, a dimension of eternal life shared by all others. In a different respect, many civilizations established hierarchical paradigms as a precedent with dystopian insights to exploit malicious curiosity as a direction with their brethren to indoctrinate a more manipulated Four Veils with abstract mystical ideologies for domination. In the force of established doctrines, a belief in assurance with false intent of faith is also instilled as a religion, exploiting itself as the only absolute means of return to eternal life and faith in God, as no one religion is to be absolute. Such exploitations led to the greater destruction of humanity's freedom in belief for an unjustified ideology, becoming known as holy wars throughout all millennia, a means of cultural annihilation. God has no legions nor an army exploiting the death of absolution in his name, nor ever shall. These unjust humanitarian actions ended many mortal journeys of spiritual souls that now must return at other times for other manifested journeys. The particular perverse theological, ideological falsehoods compelled evangelical dystopian egoism for dominance evolved as a societal mannerism amongst the populous. This alone imposed the direction of one's belief in God, not the intended truth of God, for this observance continued through the millennial evolution of civilizations. Therefore, to humankind, lay down thy swords of indoctrinated rituals of guilted dominance, request Yahweh's forgiveness and truth of tendency in his intended vibrations of pleasantries in the true faith of God within you.

Accept this, your mortal journey with grace as manifested. God's children were sent to gain knowledge and contribute to humanity's evolution through the millennium for its betterment and guardianship. For all of God's children, spiritual souls loaned to the mortal human journey of life shall transcend home for eternal healing, leaving the demised mortal body on Earth in a position of decomposition to continue its process of Earth's nurturing. So, likewise, the archangels and angels of the eternal dimensional world shall heal the spiritual soul of all that imposed unpleasantness of imposed inconceivable guilts and judgments from the soul's mortal journey.

Our mortal human life shall be lived as God manifested in reasons not made clear once born into the environment of humanity, rather made vibrant in times to come with guidance and the gain of knowledge to become your conscious wisdom in faith.

Therefore, thou shalt always understand that such a journey ends at a time when this mortal life's manifest is fulfilled.

Then, your given spiritual soul shall transcend with the assistance of angels to the dominical eternal life known as heaven. Therefore, go forth in loving peace, for the silence of your smiles shall be heard.

"Carpe animam spiritualem in corde tuo"

"Seize the spiritual soul within your heart."

Acknowledgement

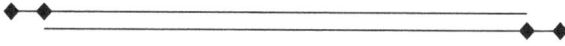

*T*he following interesting references confirmed one's thoughts on life, death, spirituality, and human ancestry, reading wonderful subject matters with great enjoyment. Each author explained the meaning of their ideological conceptual meanings in anthropology, paleontology, and theistic philosophical theories toward humanity and the civilizations of the times. The authors present a meaningful, thoughtful, and defining understanding of life, spirituality, and humanitarianism. I encourage all to read and study these references for a more precise personal interpretation. In this writing, there is no intent to change one's heartened faith in God or spiritual soul, as each feels the vibration and senses the realism of an imposed imaginary ideology of religious dominant destruction in the cause of humanity's civilizations. There is no guarantee of the clarity of ideological translations one may encounter in different language inflections and philosophies from the references conveying idealistic similarities, or in the presentation itself. The orthodox written scriptures were ministered by many philosophers thought to be disciples of God for the actual teaching of everyday life. To understand your origins and those of one's faith is pleasing to the spiritual soul in your heart and mind; further understanding of many other fascists in faiths shall continue your soul-searching for wisdom in understanding the truths of all humanity.

References

1. 1177 B.C. The Year Civilization Collapsed, by Eric H. Cline

2. Talmud of Immanuel, by Judas Ischarioth

3. The Christ of India, by Abbot George Burke (Swami Nirmalananda Giri)

4. The Kybalion, by Three Initiates, 1912, William Walker Atkinson

5. The Devil's Delusion, by David Berlinski

6. The Unknown Life of Jesus Christ, by Nicolas Notovitch

7. The Divine Pymander, by Hermes Trismegistus

8. The Secret Teachings of All Ages, by Manly P. Hall

9. They Walked With Jesus, by Dolores Cannon

10. Jesus and The Essenes, by Dolores Cannon

11. The Biology of Belief, by Bruce H. Lipton, Ph.D.

12. Paul Wallis, author and speaker of Biblical and Celestial studies.

13. Mauro Biglow, Vatican Bible Translator and author

14. The Life You Were Born To Live, by Dan Millman

15. Rabi Manis Freidman, podcast ministry.

16. Pavamana Mantra, Brihadaranyaka Upanishad

17. The Enneads, Plotinus

18. The Wisdom Codes, Gregg Braden

19. The Qur'an, by Abdullah Yusuf Ali. Surah 30: The Romans 80

20. The Jesus Hoax, by David Skrbina, Ph.D.

21. Who Wrote the Bible? Richard Elliott Friedman

22. The Tibetan Book of Living and Dying, by Sogyal Rinpoche

23. A History Of God, by Karen Armstrong

24. Religion Explained, by Pascal Boyer

25. In the Footsteps of Eve, by Lee R. Berger, Ph. D.

26. The Moral Animal, by Robert Wright

27. The New Evolutionary Timetable, by Steven M. Stanley

28. Miller-Urey Experiment, Oparin-Haldane Hypothesis

A Letter to the Creator

"Spiritual Father of all."

With all my spiritual soul, heart, and body, I express my gratitude for the impermanent spiritual mortal journey I walked through in this life, so manifested for me. I followed in the life steps of my forefathers and brethren as a seer to voice the truth of your words, asserting peaceful and emotional comfort. For all be it true, your spiritual acceptance as our creator, "Spiritual Father of all." All thou hast created, the beauty giveth in nature for us as nourishment, and the enlightenment of my gifted spiritual soul bestowed within me for this journey. In the millennia of human civilizations, I have observed the triviality in ministered words of different theistic philosophies systematized and manipulated into insidious indoctrinated apologetic commands of superiority for domination in a darker, hegemonic world disguised in theistic ideology falsehoods. If I had been adherent to these religions, I could not have believed in you as you desired, but only when commanded as to how and where to speak their belief.

With the strength of my inner spiritual faith, at the end of this journey, my knowledge will be valued with wisdom as I transcend upon my return, rendering humanity's unwarranted judgments and quilts of mortal life and reentering the eternal dimension we all share gracefully with you. In my divine heart, I have accomplished each manifested task you deemed upon me for this journey, and I give praise in my prayers unto thee.

Blessed be thy name

"Weep, not for me, for I am free with my spiritual conviction."

"Our Creator's assurance is the eternal dimension is not a magistrate nor a place of decisions for one's moment in a contemporary mortal life as a spiritual soul's journey, for there is no such ideology called judgment. Judgments are human social institutions to provoke an imposed guilt for an acceptance of an ideological indoctrination upon an individual or society for domination."

Strive to bring back the God in yourselves to the Divine in the Universe.

PLOTINUS

www.ingramcontent.com/pod-product-compliance
Lightning Source LLC
Chambersburg PA
CBHW021505090426
42739CB00007B/477